Fisher Press

NICHOLAS WISEMAN

Nicholas Wiseman was born in 1802 in Seville where his father was a merchant. Both sides of his family had their roots in Ireland. While an infant his mother consecrated him to the service of the Church in Seville Cathedral. After his father's early death his mother returned to Ireland, but she sent him at the age of eight to board in England at Ushaw College in Co. Durham. Here he was treated with favour by Dr. Lingard, the Vice Rector, who was already researching for his magisterial *History of England*.

At the age of sixteen he was one of the small party of students sent to Rome to study at the Venerable English College after its restoration by Pius VII. He gained his Doctorate after the usual public disputation, and because of his high linguistic and scholastic abilities won an open competition for the post of Professor of Oriental Languages at the University of Rome. He was frequently received by Pius VII, and at the age of twenty-six was appointed Rector of the English College. His hugely popular lectures in London in 1835 and 1836 on the Catholic Faith, given largely to Protestant audiences, brought him national fame. In 1850 he was made a Cardinal and chosen by Pius IX to restore the ecclesiastical hierarchy in England. When he took up office Catholics were still largely a persecuted sect; by the time of his death in 1865 they had come to be accepted as members of a Church which was playing an increasingly significant role in national life.

Despite his episcopal duties Cardinal Wiseman continued to pursue his scholarly and artistic interests. In 1854 he published a successful novel, *Fabiola*, about early Christians in Rome, and in 1858 his *Recollections of the Last Four Popes and of Rome in their Times*.

Published by Fisher Press, Post Office Box 41,
Sevenoaks, Kent TN15 6YN, England

The text of *Gregory XVI* was first published in 1858
as part of
Nicholas Wiseman's
*Recollections of the Last Four Popes
and of Rome in their Times*

First published as a Fisher paperback 2006

All rights reserved
Cover picture: © Tate, London
Introduction © Rev Richard Whinder

No part of this publication may be reproduced, stored in a retrieval system, or transmitted, in any form or by any means, electronic, mechanical, photocopying, recording or otherwise, without the prior permission of Fisher Press.

This book is sold subject to the condition that it shall not, by way of trade or otherwise, be lent, re-sold, hired out or otherwise circulated without the publisher's prior consent in any form of binding or cover other than in which it is published and without a similar condition being imposed on the subsequent purchaser.

British Library Cataloguing in Publication Data

A catalogue record for this book is available from
The British Library

ISBN 1 874037 19 1

NICHOLAS WISEMAN

GREGORY
THE SIXTEENTH

Fisher Press

ACKNOWLEDGEMENTS

We are grateful to the Reverend Richard Whinder for writing the Introduction to this the third and final volume of Wiseman's *Recollections of the Last Four Popes*, and for his research and assistance in producing the expanded footnotes. His interest in Gregory XVI and in Cardinal Wiseman's work was developed while he was studying at the Venerable English College in Rome.

We are also grateful to the Rev Canon John Bailey, KHS, who drew our attention to Cardinal Wiseman's prayer for the conversion of England and Wales, once regularly used in this country at Benediction and Exposition of the Blessed Sacrament. It seemed appropriate to reprint this in an Annex to his recollections of Gregory XVI, the great 19th century promoter of the Church's missionary endeavour. Pope Gregory looked forward to the restoration of the episcopal hierarchy in the mission field which this country then was. Our thanks are also due to the Very Rev Robert Byrne Cong. Orat., and Fr Dominic Jacob Cong. Orat., both of the Oxford Oratory, for their assistance with some biographical details of Fr Theiner, a some time Oratorian.

NOTE ON THIS EDITION

Readers of today may well be unfamiliar with many people and events to which Cardinal Wiseman refers. We have therefore expanded his footnotes and made some additions. Annex A contains separate short biographical sketches on a number of the most significant ecclesiastics and laymen to whom Wiseman refers. The first mention of those for whom a sketch is provided is marked with an asterisk to indicate this. There is no separate sketch on those for whom Wiseman himself provides extensive biographical detail (eg Cardinal Angelo Mai, Père Géramb and Gregory XVI himself).

Annex B contains Wiseman's prayer for the conversion of England, and Annex C a full list of Gregory XVI's encyclicals. There is also a fully comprehensive Index.

INTRODUCTION

Bartolomeo Alberto Cappellari, the future Gregory XVI, was born at Belluno, near Venice, on the 8th of September 1765. His family came from the minor nobility of what was then a territory ruled by the Republic of Venice: his family had at various times distinguished themselves in the service of the state. As a youth of 18, Bartolomeo decided to pursue a religious vocation. There was some slight opposition from his family, who presumably wished him to exercise his talents in the secular sphere, but in 1783 he entered the austere Camaldolese order,[1] taking the religious name of Mauro. The formative years of his life were thus to be spent at the monastery of San Michele di Murano, in the heart of the Venetian lagoon. Surrounded by the silence and the silvery mists, Mauro Cappellari seems to have acquired a typically Venetian love of water, which was to stay with him as Pope, as well as becoming a devout and observant Camaldolese.

In 1787 the young monk was ordained priest, and since he showed signs of considerable intellect, was put to teach philosophy at San Michele, where he showed himself an admirer of St Thomas Aquinas. From there he moved to serve in the Holy Office at Venice, and in 1795 was sent to Rome. He was thus serving at the very heart of the Church when the turbulent events of the French Revolution and the subsequent invasion of Italy took place. There can be no doubt that this revolutionary turmoil left a lasting impression on Cappellari's mind, no less than the silence and stillness of San Michele in his youth. For our purposes it is enough to note that in 1799, the very year that Pope Pius VI died in exile and apparent defeat at Valence, a

1. The canonisation of the 11th century Camaldolese Cardinal Peter Damian was a highlight of Leo XII's reign. The young Bartolomeo was following the footsteps of St Peter Orsoleo, Venetian Doge who turned Camaldolese monk in the 10th century.

prisoner of Napoleon, Cappellari published his most famous work, *Il Trionfo della Santa Sede*, or to give it its full title, *The Triumph of the Holy See and of the Church against the Assaults of the Innovators*. The book was, on the one hand, a magnificent act of faith at a time when things had rarely looked darker for the Papacy, and a splendid act of defiance to the Church's enemies. It was also, as Wiseman notes in this volume, a work of theology which was to have considerable influence on Catholic theology in the decades to come (and, after Wiseman's death, influenced the Declaration of the Dogma of Papal Infallibility in 1870), while its title eloquently revealed the outlook of its author.

The next years of Cappellari's life, his service to Pius VII, Pius VIII and Leo XII are all described in the body of this work by Wiseman, culminating in his election to the Holy See on the 2nd of February 1831, an event which, in Wiseman's touching phrase, did not alter "that amiability and simplicity of character which I had so often experienced." Leaving it to Wiseman, then, to describe the character of Pope Gregory and the great events of his reign, we will attempt what was impossible for our author in 1858, namely, to place the reign of this Pope in its historical context, and to make some assessment of its lasting impact.

To many historians, Gregory's pontificate can be summed up simply as failure, indeed, not only failure but almost as an embarrassment to the Holy See. Thus *The Oxford Dictionary of Popes* characterises the pope as "good-hearted but obstinate and narrow, with little comprehension of the modern world," and concludes "he left his successor a grievous legacy."[1] Other writers have been even more extreme in their opinion.

Gregory was certainly unfortunate with what today we would call his 'public relations.' In his lifetime he was lampooned by the writer and political figure D'Azeglio* (who penned some particularly scatological verses on the

1. J. N. D. Kelly (ed), *The Oxford Dictionary of Popes*, Oxford, 1998.

INTRODUCTION

Pontiff's death). Certain personality traits made him particularly easy to mock and to caricature. For instance his notorious hatred of railways, alluded to by Wiseman, has been held up for general ridicule. We shall consider below whether Gregory's 'reactionary,' attitude to certain aspects of civil government may have had some serious purpose. For the moment, it should simply be noted that Gregory himself almost saw the humour in the situation. His most famous comment on railways, when he dubbed them '*chemin d'infer*' (ways of hell), was clearly intended as a joke, playing on the French for railway, *chemin de fer* (ways of steel). He knew that their coming was inevitable and ruefully acknowledged that they would enter the Papal States once he was '*sotto la terra*' (ie, dead).

One of the facts which comes out from Wiseman's *Recollections*, and has been studiously ignored by most other historians, is that Gregory was a man of considerable humour and charm. He even mocked his own status as a theologian, remarking self-deprecatingly to the historian, Jacques Cretineau-Joly*, "Do you know that I have written a splendid book, *Il Trionfo della Santa Sede*? At first nobody talked about it, not even my brethren in the convent. But now that I am Pope, everybody is agreed it is a remarkable work."[1]

This sense of humour and lack of self-importance often stood him in good stead. For instance, he was once accosted by an Englishwoman who had travelled all the way to Rome to upbraid the Vicar of Christ with his pride for claiming the charism of Infallibility. She obtained an audience and duly delivered her rebuke. Gregory heard her out with great politeness, acknowledged the importance of humility and admitted his own sinfulness, for which, as he said, he begged forgiveness of God before the altar every day. But, he added, had his accuser herself not considered whether she might stand in need of greater humility? The lady, we are told, was much impressed with the pope's reaction, and later entered the

---

1. Frederik Nielsen, *The Papacy in the XIXth Century*, London, 1906, p. 54.

Catholic Church.[1]

We also hear of Gregory halting Papal processions in order to stop and chat with small children (his Master of Ceremonies disapproved) and when a certain town erected a triumphal arch fashioned from grapes to honour the pontiff, the embarrassed Gregory had the structure dismantled and distributed to the poor.[2] He remained, in fact, a simple monk at heart, and whenever possible he liked to spend his time touring in the Castelli Romani, the string of small cities to the south of Rome, which were, in his time, almost untouched by revolution and modernity. Here he spent his time conversing with parish priests and simple friars or, when his travels took him to the Papal villa at Castelgandolfo, he would fish for hours in a small boat on the Alban Lake (the legacy of his Venetian youth). He delighted also in the water-games installed in the Papal gardens by his Eighteenth Century predecessors, and took great pleasure in dousing his courtiers and familiars with their concealed jets of water. He had restored to full working order the water-organ which Clement VIII had placed in the gardens of the Quirinal Palace, and there the Pope and some of his favoured Cardinals would gather to listen to the strains of Italian opera, while eating *bon-bons* sent specially from France.[3]

Finally, and on a more scholarly note, we should remember that it was Gregory who founded the Etruscan and Egyptian museums at the Vatican, which continue to delight visitors to this day.

All this goes to show that Gregory XVI had a very human heart. He was no monster. Neither was he an idiot or an ignoramus. He was, on the other hand, unquestionably conservative. He was born under the *ancien régime*, in a

---

1. A story told in Edward O'Gorman, *Our Islands and Rome*, London, 1974.
2. See M. Rinaldi and M. Vicini, *Buon Appetito Santità*, Publigold, Italy 1998.
3. H. V. Morton, *The Water of Rome*, George Rainbird Ltd, London, 1966.

INTRODUCTION

class which had most to lose from the Revolution. His first-hand experience of the events in Rome under Pius VI and Pius VII had left him with the understandable conviction that the agents of social change were inevitably the enemies of the Church. And, as Wiseman makes clear, the rebellions which broke out in various parts of the Papal States at the time of Gregory's election—while not aimed at him personally—poisoned the atmosphere of his reign, and left it tainted with the air of repression. Since no real papal army existed, Gregory was forced to rely on the armed forces of Austria in putting down the insurrection. The Austrians then remained for some time, effectively an occupying force for which the citizens of the Papal States were obliged to pay heavy taxes—an extremely awkward (if inevitable) situation, as Wiseman himself seems to infer.

Gregory, then, had little room for manoeuvre politically. On the other hand, he continued the policy of his predecessors in governing the Church itself without interference from the secular powers, and here he showed the extent to which he was prepared to change and adapt for the good of the Faith.

Gregory's priority—and perhaps his greatest legacy—was the missionary activity of the Church. Under Leo XII he had served as Cardinal-Prefect for *Propaganda Fide*, the Vatican Congregation charged with promoting the foreign missions, and he chose the name 'Gregory,' chiefly to honour the memory of Gregory XV, who had founded *Propaganda Fide*.[1] Despite having lived a relatively enclosed life as a Camaldolese monk, Gregory seemed to have an instinctive grasp of the importance of the missions, and his achievements in this field were considerable.

During his Pontificate new mission fields opened up in Abyssinia, India, China, North America (among the indigenous peoples) and in Polynesia, all with the Pope's active support. We should note in this context that in order

1. The name Gregory also recalled Pope St Gregory the Great, founder of the Abbey of San Gregorio al Coelio, where the future Gregory XVI was abbot from 1805.

to further the spread of the Gospel abroad, Gregory was prepared to act against his own very conservative political leanings. We see this most clearly in the case of South America. Here, a spate of nationalist revolutions had thrown off the yoke of Portugal and Spain. Both as Prefect of Propaganda, and later as Pope, Gregory enthusiastically backed the policy of appointing bishops for these newly independent states, although this could be seen as the Church giving its blessing to a revolution (and risked incurring the wrath of the Imperial powers).

His attitude towards Louis-Philippe of France is also illuminating. Louis-Philippe had come to the throne in 1830, when revolution overthrew the last Bourbon, Charles X, a conservative and a strong Catholic. Gregory's own sympathies, clearly, were with Charles, and he allowed this to show in his dealings with the French in Rome. Nevertheless, he made no public show of support for the Bourbons, and went as far as to say: "The Church is the friend of all governments, provided they do not trample upon liberty. I am very well satisfied with Louis-Philippe: I wish all the sovereigns of Europe were like him."[1] In 1831, one of Gregory's first acts was to issue the Bull *Sollicitudo Ecclesiarum*, which stated as an article of policy that the Holy See would follow its traditional practise and deal with *de facto* governments, without entering into abstract questions of right, and this is precisely the course which he himself followed.[2]

If Gregory was prepared to repress his own instincts in order to further the Church's missionary efforts, he showed similar spirit in adapting the Papacy itself to modern needs. Doubtless the shy, scholarly Camaldolese would have found some solace if he had been pope in the eighteenth century when pontiffs could either live simply, or devote themselves

1. Nielsen, *op. cit.* p. 89.
2. Another important Bull of Gregory, for which he is almost never given credit, is *In Supremo Apostolatus fastigio* of 1839, which condemned slavery and the slave trade as 'utterly unworthy of the Christian name.' A full list of Gregory's encyclicals is at Annex C.

INTRODUCTION

to the arts, or even live in some style, provided they were benign and accessible, and left the Church and society as they found them. Instead, he came to the throne of Peter at a time of social and ecclesiastical upheaval, and when the burgeoning Ultramontane movement was bringing the person of the pope more and more into the foreground. Gregory did his best to respond. He made the most of events such as the consecration of the re-built basilica of St Paul Without-the-Walls.[1] He embarked on a tour of the Papal States to meet his subjects (although this was not altogether successful) and was apparently the first Pope to be photographed.[2] In all these fields of 'popular' activity, Gregory's example was to be followed, and altogether exceeded, by his charming and saintly successor, Blessed Pius IX—a man who had the common touch Gregory sadly lacked.

More importantly, Gregory also exploited a form of Papal outreach which, again, was to be of immense advantage to his successors—the Papal Encyclical Letter. Scholars dispute as to which Papal missive can claim to be the first encyclical in history—the First Epistle of St Peter and the *Epistola encyclica et commonitoria* on the duties of the Episcopate issued by Benedict XIV in 1746 are sometimes cited — but Gregory pioneered the genre in its modern form. *Mirari vos* (1832) and *Singulari nos* (1834) are just two of his most famous encyclicals, and illustrate the way in which the new medium was used. They gave a swift, authoritative answer to pressing issues, exercising the papal ministry internationally and in a manner well-adapted to the Nineteenth century, with its rapid change and global

1. The rebuilt basilica claimed an admirer in no less a person than Henry James, who wrote: "The restored Basilica is simply splendid...It rises there, gorgeous and useless, on its miasmic site, with an air of conscious bravado—a florid advertisement of the superabundance of faith." H. James, *Italian Hours*, London 1909.
2. According to the catalogue for the exhibition *Papi in posi* (Museo di Roma, November 2004—to February 2005). The picture was taken at the Jesuit house at Tivoli, but was not displayed in the exhibition.

communications. In *Il Trionfo della Santa Sede* Gregory had discerned the importance of a vigorous Papacy in defending the Church's interests in a changing world. The Encyclical Letter has proved an enduring vehicle for the Papal voice to be heard. (see Annex C for a full list of his encyclicals.)

This brings us back to Gregory's attitude towards civil government, in particular, to his government of the city of Rome. If he was ready to embrace new developments in the way the papacy worked, why did he set his heart against change in the secular world?

There are various arguments to consider. Firstly, as Wiseman makes clear, Gregory did in fact follow the example of Leo XII, and endeavoured to make some improvements in the civil government of his states. Thus, a national bank was set up in the Papal States for the first time, a decimal currency introduced, chambers of commerce established in various cities and several important public works undertaken in Rome—even Nielsen commends his efforts to stamp out cholera. As Antony Matthew makes clear, in his introduction to the second volume of Wiseman's *Recollections*, we should be wary of adopting too hastily the dismissive attitude of Nineteenth Century liberal visitors to Rome, who ridiculed everything they found as backward and archaic. Anglo-Saxons, especially, arrived with an in-built Protestant bias against all things Roman, and unfairly contrasted the Papal States—a small, largely agrarian economy—with the growing industrial powerhouse that was Victorian Britain.

Nevertheless, we can accept that Gregory's policy to government in his territories—and to Rome in particular—was certainly backward-looking. His attitude to railways and gas lighting for the streets became notorious (he opposed both). Similarly, in terms of the etiquette of the Papal court, and small details of liturgical and civil ceremonies, Gregory invariably clung to the traditions of the past (Pius IX was to prove an unlikely innovator in some of these matters). Why was this so?

INTRODUCTION

Firstly, we must remember that the popes for decades had opposed developing Rome along the lines of other modern cities, and we need to realise that in doing so they were not acting as reactionary tyrants but rather reflecting the authentic voice of the Roman people. In a fascinating recent book, Susan Vandiver Nicassio shows the reader the lifestyle, attitudes and aspirations of the ordinary citizen in early Nineteenth Century Rome, allowing us to hear a voice far too easily forgotten.[1] She notes that innovations which to us seem obviously beneficial—for instance, street lighting—were almost universally opposed by the populace, because they appeared as an alien, 'official,' intrusion into what was considered private property (the Roman street at this period was not so much a public thoroughfare as a mere extension of the houses along it, and could often serve as bedroom, bathroom, kitchen and workplace).

Nicassio points out that many supposed 'improvements,' carried out by the French during the Napoleonic occupation of Rome —for instance, imposing street names and numbering the houses—in reality acted as instruments of oppression, allowing the citizens to be 'organised,' for the purposes of taxation and military conscription. The Roman people remembered, and resented, this. Moreover, their sense of identity, which sprang from family ties and a proud feeling of continuity with the wonders of ancient Rome, tended to make them suspicious of state interference, and opposed to anything which would alter the unique character of their birth place.

To these considerations we can add another. There was, it seems, always something a little quixotic about Pope Gregory's character. He chose the year the papacy had sunk to its lowest ebb to publish a book entitled *The Triumph of the Holy See*, and it is tempting to see a similar defiance in his determination to keep the city of Rome aloof from the changes all around it.

1. *Imperial City: Rome, Romans and Napoleon, 1795-1815*, Ravenhall Books, 2005.

This is even more the case when we consider that he obviously knew—and admitted—that change would come eventually. But by then Gregory would have made his point.

The conservatism of the city of Rome was a statement, flung in the face of the liberals and modernisers who decried her old fashioned ways, while they nevertheless flocked there in droves. Rome might not have the good drainage of other cities, might lack fast roads, modern factories, gas lighting and an efficient civil service—but she stood for something else. In Rome, where the only light after sunset came from the lamps which flickered before the street shines, where on Good Friday the Papal troops muffled their drums in honour of the buried Christ, and where even a condemned criminal could not be put to death until the Confraternity of St John-the-Beheaded had ensured that he had made his confession and set his soul at peace, men were everywhere reminded of their eternal destiny. And this was especially the case for those liberals and modernisers who least liked to be reminded of that destiny. Like Leo XII's Holy Year of 1825,[1] Gregory's preservation of 'Old Rome,' was a deliberate affront to much of what the modern world stood for—and a defiant re-assertion of Catholic principles.

Before we leave the subject, it is worth noting that when Rome finally did change—and it changed dramatically following the Piedmontese occupation of 1870 and the declaration of a United Italy with Rome as its capital—people suddenly began to realise what they had lost. This was especially the case for those foreign visitors—Anglo-Saxons in particular—who had previously gone to lament the supposed backwardness of the Romans and bewail the incompetence of the papal government. It was as if Gregory XVI had been posthumously vindicated.

Nor was it just those travellers who knew Rome best

1. For a full account of the Papal Jubilee of 1825 see *Leo XII and Pius VIII*, Fisher Press, 2005, pp. 38-48.

INTRODUCTION

and sympathised most with her people—those such as F. Marion Crawford[1] and Augustus Hare[2]—who lamented the diminution of her unique character, but even writers who deprecated the popes and Catholicism in general, had to admit that something special had been lost. Thus even Mrs Humphry Ward, in her 'Roman novel,' of 1900, *Eleanor*, has to admit that the end of the old regime has led to the destruction of much that was picturesque and beautiful, even as she celebrates the onward march of 'progress.' Nevertheless, Ward dedicated her novel to "Italy, the beloved and beautiful," and addressed the country optimistically as "instructress of our past, delight of our present, comrade of our future."

Sadly Ward had failed to predict that within a few years of her novel, early Twentieth Century Italy would have collapsed under the weight of venal government and aggressive militarism, and would eventually surrender to the evils of totalitarianism. Others, who took a more realistic view of Italian nationalism, were more prescient.[3]

1. Francis Marion Crawford (1854-1909). Prolific novelist and journalist, and a convert to Catholicism. He had spent his youth in Rome, and knew the city like few other English speaking writers.
2. Augustus Hare (1834-1903). English writer and raconteur. His *Walks in Rome* and *Days near Rome* were, and remain, much loved guides to the city. The latter contains this splendid lament for the passing of 'Old Rome': "While acknowledging certain beneficial changes introduced by the present Government, it is not only the artist who will recognise that much of interest, and as much as possible of the beauty, of the 'Eternal City' has been destroyed. Not only has all trace of costume perished, together with the medieval figures and splendid dresses that belonged to the Papal Court, and walked in footsteps of crimson cardinals; but all the gorgeous religious ceremonies, all the processions, and benedictions, and sermons preached by the shrines of martyrs, have ceased to exist. Even the time-honoured Pifferari (Ed. traditional bagpipers from the Abruzzi mountains) have been chased from Rome by the present Government as a public nuisance..."
3. For example, F M Crawford. His novel of 1896, *Taquisara*, contains this vivid warning about the path on which Italy was set: "That Italy has done what she has done in thirty years, to be a power among nations, is a marvel, and almost a miracle. That she should have ever done it at all, is the great-

This mention of the Twentieth Century, and the evils which were to beset it, brings us to the final aspect of Gregory XVI's reign we must consider—namely his confrontation with modern thought, particularly as represented by the figure of Félicité de Lamennais*.

This is a controversial area, since the condemnation of Lamennais foreshadowed the censure of the Modernists in the early Twentieth century, and other Papal interventions since. It is not helped by the complexity of the arguments, which have often been misunderstood and misrepresented.

Lamennais, like the founder of Twentieth Century Modernism, Alfred Loisy, eventually died an excommunicate, but there is no reason to doubt that at the time of his initial condemnation in 1832, Lamennais was a fervent Catholic and sincerely desired to serve the Church. Indeed, no one ever denied this, least of all Gregory XVI. It was not the young priest's intentions that were suspected—but the unseen implications of his thinking.

Lamennais' genius had been to turn post-Revolutionary Europe's weapons against itself, accepting the new ideas of liberty, but demanding the right to use that liberty in the service of the Church. Thus, where Catholicism had traditionally been seen as an ally of absolute monarchs, Lamennais indicated his support for democracy—sensing that, in an age where the great majority of people still practised their Christian faith, the popular vote might actually be used to shore up the authority of the Church against its enemies. Similarly, where the Church had always been prepared to support the use of censorship—particularly for works of immorality or political subversion—Lamennais supported the calls for a free press. However, that freedom of the press would include the right for Catholics to publish whatever they wished—even if it

est mistake ever committed by a civilised nation, and it is irrevocable, as its results are to be fatal and lasting. But upon the good reality of unity, the deadly dream of military greatness descended as a killing blight, and the evil vision of political power has blasted the common sense of a whole people...."

was offensive to atheists, rationalists and freethinkers. Thus Lamennais made a name for himself as the great champion of Liberty and Catholicism, and for a while had great success. Leo XII feted him, and for a while even considered making him a cardinal (as recounted in *Leo XII & Pius VIII*, the second volume of Wiseman's *Recollections*).

Trouble, however, was not long in coming. Lamennais soon made powerful enemies politically, and before long theologically as well. To understand Lamennais' theology, we need to realise that he was responding to the attacks on Catholicism that had been made in the Enlightenment period. Then, the Rationalists and their friends had cast doubt on the traditional arguments for the existence of God, claiming to act in the name of reason. Rather than seeking to refute these arguments systematically, Lamennais turned the attack on reason itself, and sought to justify the faith on a new basis, one which accorded with his democratic instincts and with the Romanticism of the early Nineteenth Century. History showed, he believed, that the individual reason was incapable of reaching certitude, whether about religious matters or anything else. However, God could be found in another way. Lamennais appealed instead to the deepest-seated instincts of the human race, what he called the *sens commun*, "the authoritative consent of humanity, from which acceptance God's existence at once follows...the very principle of human knowledge and certitude."[1]

Lamennais was careful to find a role in this theory for the Pope, who became "the universal pastor...the organ of this enhanced *sens commun*, the voice of the tradition of the people."[2] Indeed, Lamennais was an early Ultramontane, and sought the support of the papacy against the suspicions of his local bishops —which was the very reason he brought his case to Rome in 1831.

1. Aidan Nichols OP, *Catholic Thought since the Enlightenment*, Gracewing, Leominster, 1998.
2. Ibid.

Nielsen, in his *History*, portrays the condemnation of Lamennais as a crudely political manoeuvre, and Gregory as the dupe of the French Monarchists, who opposed Lamennais for his support of democracy. But this interpretation fails to fit the facts. Firstly, although the monarchists played their part, Lamennais' most vehement opponents were the recently re-founded Jesuits, who championed the older, neo-scholastic theology. They had particular problems with Lamennais' teachings on the place of reason and the gratuity of faith. Nielsen's interpretation also ignores the fact that Gregory was himself an accomplished theologian, more than capable of seeing the theological objections to Lamennais' theories, even apart from political considerations. Nor can it be denied that the objections to this new theology were indeed well-founded, from a Catholic point of view.

Firstly, in abandoning the role of reason and appealing instead to the subjective authority of the *sens commun*, Lamennais opened the way to relativism in matters of religious doctrine. True, he had attempted to find a role for the papacy within his system, but the speed with which he himself abandoned his allegiance to Rome, following the condemnation of 1831, shows the perilous path he was on.

Secondly, and perhaps even more seriously, there were the social consequences of Lamennais' doctrine. Traditionally, Catholic theology, and social teaching, had taken account of the inestimable value of the individual soul, as well as insisting that human societies could, with the aid of reason, discover the proper path for human conduct laid down by God.[1] Lamennais, on the contrary, sought to found a new social order, based not on individual dignity or the claims of reason, but on the collective, non-rational will of virile societies, which were to be whipped into action by the preaching of charismatic prophets such as himself. In his

---

1. For an elegant and humane defence of the traditional Catholic principles of individual dignity, the importance of family and property, the rule of law and "the infinite and merciful gradations of a hierarchical society," see *The Commonplace Book of Monsignor A. N. Gilbey*, London, 1993.

INTRODUCTION

Paroles d'un Croyant, for instance, which followed his condemnation in the encyclical *Mirari vos*, Lamennais called for the overthrow of the existing order, which he described as a conspiracy of priests and kings against the people. In these writings lay the seed of those poisonous doctrines which were to cause such trouble for Europe in the late Nineteenth and Twentieth Centuries. Non-rational, revolutionary ideologies such as nationalism, militarism and totalitarianism in its various hues, could all seek support in the thinking of Lamennais. Indeed, this aspect of its thought found its clearest development in the philosophy of Nietzsche, for whom the social order of the future was to be, in the words of the philosopher Roger Scruton, "a new world, in which human institutions will be no longer shored up by pious habits and holy doctrines, but rebuilt from the raw, untempered fabric of the will to power."[1]

Little wonder that Gregory XVI should have opposed such thinking, or reacted with such horror to the *Paroles d'un Croyant*, which he described in the encyclical *Singulari nos* as "a book small in size but immense in perversity." Throughout this whole controversy, indeed, Gregory's language glows with a strange fervour. Reading *Mirari vos*, one could imagine that the pope had had some inkling of the horror that lay in the future, when Europe would indeed cast off the Christian yoke, and attempt to build itself anew on those strange philosophies of which Lamennais was an unwitting prophet: "For since all restraint has been removed by which men are kept on the paths of truth, since their nature inclined to evil is now plunging headlong, we say that 'the bottom of the pit' has truly been opened, from which John saw 'smoke rising by which the sun was darkened with locusts coming out of it to devastate the earth.' "

The last years of Gregory's reign were marked by growing tensions in the Papal States, with an increasing threat of revolution. Gregory himself—an old man now, and given to brooding—blamed much of the trouble on the secret soci-

---

1. Roger Scruton, *Gentle Regrets: Thoughts from a Life*, London, 2005.

eties, the Freemasons and *carbonari*[1] and commissioned his friend, the historian Cretineau-Joly, to write a history of these societies from papers he had collected. Cretineau-Joly began the work, but it was subsequently abandoned during the reign of Pius IX, who judged it inopportune.

At the end of May 1846, Gregory suddenly became extremely ill. His courtiers did not imagine him to be in imminent danger, but on the 1st of June he died, alone and in great pain. Like Leo XII before him, he had been a man of personal austerity, and he had refused to summon physicians because he wanted to spare the papal coffers. The gesture was a quixotic one, like so much else in his life. He died, therefore, not in the manner of a prince, or a Sovereign Pontiff, but as a poor man, a sad but strangely appropriate death for a man who, as a youth of eighteen, had sought the poverty and obscurity of a Camaldolese cloister.

History was unkind to him, and posterity has heaped scorn on his memory, but at the time he was widely mourned, and the Romans queued to kiss the feet of the dead pope, as he lay in silent state before the Altar of the Blessed Sacrament in St Peter's. Wiseman too must have mourned him, for he was, as this memoir eloquently shows, not just a spiritual father to Wiseman, but a friend. In these pages, therefore, we get to see a glimpse of Gregory XVI as he really was, in all his humanity, his warmth and his goodness. The book is a fitting epitaph to a pope who has been much misunderstood, but did much to contribute to the flourishing of the Church in the Nineteenth Century.

RICHARD WHINDER

1. *Carbonari*. Literally "charcoal-burners," a secret society originating about the time of the French revolution, with a large membership in both France and Italy. Its members promoted a purely natural and syncretistic view of religion, and worked for the overthrow of traditional monarchism. All such societies were condemned in an edict signed by Cardinals Consalvi and Pacca on 15 August 1815, and Catholics were forbidden under severe penalties to become members.

CHAPTER I

HIS CONSECRATION

"YOU must now revise your own proofs. I fear I shall not have much time in future to correct proofs." Such were the words which I heard from the mouth of Gregory XVI. They were preceded by a kind exclamation of recognition, and followed by a hearty blessing, as I knelt before him in the narrow passage leading from the private papal apartments. It was only a few days after his accession. The new Pope alluded to an act of singular kindness on his part. He had desired me to expand an essay and publish it as a little work in Italian; on a subject in which, as Prefect of Propaganda, he took an interest. It was passing through the press of that institution, and he had undertaken to correct its sheets. Throughout the duration of the conclave, down to the very eve of his election, he had persevered in this proof of condescension, and thus probably spared the future reader some amount of infelicities in diction, or inaccuracy of facts. At any rate that short interview proved to me that Gregory's elevation to the Supreme Pontificate had not altered that amiability and simplicity of character which I had already so often experienced.

The conclave after the death of Pius commenced in the middle of December, with the observance of the usual forms.[1] At one time it seemed likely to close with the election of Cardinal Giustiniani*; when the Court of Spain interposed and prevented it. Allusion has been made to the existence of this privilege,[2] vested more by usage, than by any formal act of recognition, at least in three great

---

1. For a papal conclave procedure see *Leo XII & Pius VIII*, Fisher Press, 2005, pp. 2-3, 9.2. *Ibid*, p. 7.

Catholic Powers. Should two-thirds of the votes centre in any person, he is at once Pope, beyond the reach of any prohibitory declaration. It is, therefore, when votes seem to be converging towards someone obnoxious, no matter why, to one of the sovereigns, that his ambassador to conclave, himself a Cardinal, by a circular, admonishes his colleagues of this feeling in the court which he represents. This sufficies to make them turn in another direction.

Thus at an earlier conclave before the one now before us, Cardinal Severoli* was nearly elected, when Cardinal Albani,* on behalf of Austria (Francis I), to which Severoli had been formerly Nuncio, inhibited his election, by a note considered far from courteous. And, in like manner in this conclave, on the 7th of January, Cardinal Giustiniani received twenty-one votes, the number sufficient for election being twenty-nine, when Cardinal Marco*, Spanish envoy, delicately intimated, first to Giustiniani's nephew, Odescalchi*, then to the Dean Pacca*, that Spain (Ferdinand VII) objected to that nomination. Everyone was amazed. Giustiniani had been Nuncio in Spain; and the ground of his exclusion was supposed to be, his participation in Leo XII's appointment of bishops in South America. If so, the object in view was signally defeated. For the power of veto, possessed by the crown of any country is exhausted by the first exercise; the sting remains behind in the wound. Cardinal Cappellari had been instrumental, far more than Giustiniani, in promoting those episcopal nominations, and he united the requisite number of votes, and was Pope.

Everyone in that conclave, however, bore witness to the admirable conduct of that excellent and noble prince on the occasion. I have heard Cardinal Weld*, and his secretary in conclave, Bishop Riddell, describe how wretched and pining he looked while the prospect of the papacy hung before him, for he was scrupulous and tender of conscience to excess; and how he brightened up and looked himself again, the moment the vision had passed away. Indeed, no

GREGORY THE SIXTEENTH

sooner had the note of the Spanish lay ambassador, Labrador, been read in his presence by the Dean, than Cardinal Giustiniani rose, and standing in the middle of the chapel, addressed his colleagues. He was tall, his scanty hair was white with age, his countenance peculiarly mild. His mother was an English lady, and his family are now claiming the Newburgh peerage in Scotland, from the Crown.[1]

With an unfaltering voice, and a natural tone, unagitated by his trying position, the Cardinal said: "If I did not know courts by experience, I should certainly have cause to be surprised at the 'exclusion' published by the most eminent Dean; since, far from being able to reproach myself with having given cause of complaint against me to his Catholic Majesty, during my nunciature, I dare congratulate myself with having rendered His Majesty signal service in the difficult circumstances wherein he was placed." He then referred to some proofs of acknowledgement of this fidelity from the Spanish Crown; and continued: "I will always cherish the memory of these kindnesses shown me by His Catholic Majesty, and will entertain towards him the most profound respect, and in addition a most lively interest for all that can regard his welfare, and that of his august family. I will further add, that, of all the benefits conferred on me by His Majesty, I consider the greatest and most acceptable to me (at least in its effects) to be his having this day closed for me the access to the most sublime dignity of the Pontificate. Knowing, as I do, my great weakness I could not bring myself to foresee that I should ever have to take on myself so heavy a burthen; yet these few days back, on seeing that I was thought of for this purpose, my mind has been filled with the bitterest sorrow. Today I find myself free from anxiety, I am restored to tranquility, and I retain only the gratification of knowing that some of my most worthy colleagues have deigned to cast a look on me, and have honoured me with their votes, for which I beg to offer them my eternal and sincerest gratitude."

1. It has since been obtained.

This address visibly moved the entire assembly; and many Cardinals visited Giustiniani in his cell, to express to him their admiration of his conduct and his virtues.[1]

Gregory XVI gave every proof of his esteem; and after the death of Cardinal Weld, he was named Cardinal Protector of the English College, in consideration of his English descent. This gave me many opportunties of conferring with him, and learning his genuine and solid good qualities.

It would seem as if the pontifical dignity, in modern times, had to alternate between the two ecclesiastical divisions in the Church, the secular and regular. Pius VII belonged to the latter, the two next Popes to the former class. In Cardinal Capellari a return was made to the monastic order. His three immediate predecessors had passed through certain preparatory steps; had been graced with the episcopal dignity before they reached the pontifical, had been bishops or public characters in stirring times: he had never left the cloister till he was clothed with the purple—though in his case this was but a symbolical phrase;[2] and after this, he only filled one, and that an ecclesiastical office. His previous life, therefore, may be easily sketched.

Bartholomew Albert Capellari was born at Belluno, in Lombardy, on September 18, 1765, of parents belonging to the nobles of the place. In 1783 he took the habit of the Camaldolese order, and with it assumed the name of Maurus, in the monastery of San Michele in Murano, at Venice. In 1795 he was deputed to Rome on business, and there, in 1799, he published a large work of great merit, which gave proof of his extensive and varied learning.[3] In

1. Moroni, *Dizionario*, vol., xxxi, p. 221.
2. On becoming a Cardinal, a religious preserves the colour of his habit. That of the Camaldolese being white, Gregory XVI never changed the colour of his robes, but wore the same as a monk, a cardinal, and pope.
3. It is entitled, "*Il trionfo della Santa Sede e della Chiesa, contro gli assalti dei Novatori.*" It passed through three editions in Venice, and has been translated into several languages.

1805 he was created Abbot, and exercised the office at the monastery of St Gregory in Rome, and in that of his original profession at Venice. The first, however, became his place of residence.

The church and monastery of St Gregory are beautifully situated on the Caelean hill, and occupy the site of a religious house founded by that great Pope, in his own house. Its original dedication was to the Apostle St Andrew, in whose honour there still exists a chapel in the garden, adorned with exquisite frescoes. Over the threshold of this house proceeded St Augustine, and other missioneries, whom St Gregory sent to England. From the Benedictines it passed into the hands of the Camaldolese, a branch of that religious order. The Camaldolese take their name from one of the three celebrated "Sanctuaries" of Tuscany, situated among the fastnesses of the Appenines, and remarkable for the beauty of their positions, and of the prospects around them. But the Camaldolese, founded by St Romuald in the thirteenth century, have two forms of life, one monastic, the other eremitical. The latter has been in part described, when an account was given of their abduction, by *banditti*, of a community on Tusculum[1]. It was to the monastic branch that Dom Mauro Capellari belonged. In the splendid monastery of St Gregory the Great, he passed upwards of twenty years of quiet obscurity, enjoying the command of a rich library, to which he greatly added.

But, although scarcely known to the public, he was one of the many living in Rome, who silent and unseen carry on the great business of the Church, as its counsellors, theologians, and referees in arduous affairs. In this way Father Cappellari was well known to the Holy See; and full opportunity was given him to become acquainted with ecclesiastical and even civil business, and to manifest his ability, prudence, and uprightness in its transaction. Among other grave duties, Leo XII imposed on him those

1. See *Pius VII*, Fisher Press, 2003, pp. 116-9.

of visitor of the four lesser universities. Those who knew his merits fully expected that he would be soon placed in a position to display them more usefully; when it appeared as if a friendly rival had stepped in between him and his well-earned honours.

Another religious of the same order , and from the same province, had come to Rome much later, and was his junior by several years. This was D. Placido Zurla*; a man of great learning and pleasing manners, and adorned besides with high moral qualities. But he had taken no leading part in ecclesiastical affairs in Rome, nor had he borne the weight of its evil days. His celebrity, indeed, as an author had been in a very different line, that of geographical research. In 1818 he had pubished, at Venice, an interesting work on Marco Polo and other early Venetian travellers; and he had brought to light, or at least greatly illustrated, a singular map of the world, preserved in the library of St Mark's, which, though long anterior to the age of Columbus, seemed to give hint of a western continent.

He was an intimate friend of Father Capellari; and all Rome was astonished when he was named Cardinal by Pius VII, in May, 1823, not because his own merits were underrated, but because his elevation seemed to bar that of his fellow-monk. For it was supposed to be impossible that two religious should be raised to the purple from one very limited monastic body. So Zurla felt it; and on receiving notice of his coming nomination, he is said to have proceeded to the feet of Pius, and deprecated it, as an injustice to his friend—indeed, as certainly a mistake. However, it was not so. He became Vicar of Rome, and was Protector of our college till his death in Sicily in 1834. Not the slightest interruption of affection ever took place between the two religious brethren, even after the last had become first; and Zurla was vicar to Capellari.

In fact, Leo XII, overlooking all usages, ordered a complete equipment for a cardinal to be prepared at his own charge; and the colour and form of the robes left no doubt who the unknown nominee was to be.[1] On the 25th of March, 1825, Leo created Capellari Cardinal, but reserved him *in petto*, till the 13th of March of the following year, when he proclaimed him with such a *eulogium* as has seldom been pronounced in consistory. He spoke of him as a person, "very remarkable for innocence and gravity of manners, and most learned, especially in ecclesiastical matters, and for protracted labours endured for the Apostolic See."

On the Feast of the Purification, on the 2nd of February, 1831, an end was put to the conclave by the election of Cappellari to the Supreme Pontificate, by the name of Gregory. The ceremony of his coronation, which took place on the 6th, was enhanced by his consecration as Bishop, at the High Altar of St Peter's. This function served clearly to exhibit the concurrence in his person of two different orders of ecclesiastical power. From the moment of his acceptance of papal dignity, he was Supreme Head of the Church; could decree, rule, name and depose bishops, and exercise every duty of pontifical jurisdiction. But he could not ordain, nor consecrate, till he had received the imposition of hands from other bishops, inferior to himself, and holding under him their sees and jurisdiction.

On a previous occasion, when Clement XIV, was named Pope, he received episcopal consecration separately from his coronation. Gregory united the two functions; but following the still older precedent, departed from the ordinary forms.

In the Roman Pontifical, the rite prescribed for episcopal consecration is interwoven with the Mass, during which the new bishop occupies a very subordinate place till the end, when he is enthroned, and pronouces his first episcopal benediction. Here the entire rite preceded the Mass, which was sung in the usual form by the new Pope. Like every other Bishop, he recited, kneeling before the altar, and in the presence of his clergy, the Profession of Faith—the bond

---

1. Because they were white.

here which united the Head with the Body, instead of being, as ordinarily, the link which binds a member to the Head.

The morning was bright and full of joy; the evening came gloomy and charged with sinister prognostics. It was in the very square of the Vatican, while first receiving the Papal blessing, that the rumour reached us of insurrection in the provinces. It was one of those vague reports the origin and path of which no one can trace. For it was only on the 4th that Bologna had risen. A canonade had been heard in the direction of Modena, which was taken for a signal of a premature revolution. It was that of the Grand-Duke's attack on the house of Ciro Menotti, who had been treated with all the kindness of a domestic friend by that monarch, while he was the very centre of a general conspiracy. His treachery was discovered, and his intentions were frustrated by the vigilance and intrepidity of the Duke, who took, and himself conveyed him, away, captive, where he could be better held. Soon the insurrection spread; and, having occupied the legations, overflowed its original boundaries, and sent its forces towards the capital, where a movement was attempted, but with no real success.

I remember perfectly the night of February 12. It was carnival time, of the good old days, when later restrictions had not been thought of, and everyone was on pleasure bent, hearty and harmless, for the hours. On the afternoon of that day, just as the sports were going to begin,[1] an edict premptorily suspended them; troops patrolled the Corso, and other public places; and citizens were warned to remain at home, as evil-disposed persons machinated mischief. Three days before a plot had been formed for the surprise and seizure of the Fort of St Angelo; but it had been foiled by the watchfulness of the Government. In the evening of the 12th some sharp reports of fire-arms reached our ears, and told us of an

1. For a description of the sports and other apects of the Carnival in the 'good old days,' see F. Marion Crawford: *Ave Roma Immortalis*, London, 1909, pp.182-90, and Maurice Andrieux: *Daily Life in Papal Rome in the Eighteenth Century* (as translated by Mary Fitton), London, 1968, pp. 141-7.

attempt, at least, to excite a violent revolution. It was, in truth, an attack on the guard of the Post-office, with the intention of seizing its arms and ammunition. But the soldiers were on the alert; they returned the fire, wounded several, and captured many of the assailants; and all was quiet. One ball went through the gate of the Piombino Palace, and, I believe, killed the innocuous porter within.

As for ourselves, not knowing what might happen, or in what direction the blind fury of a successful rebellion might direct itself; ignorant also of the extent and resources of the aggressors; we took every precaution against nocturnal surprise. Our doors were solid, our windows well barred, our walls impregnable. After careful survey of the premises, only one weak point was discovered, not proof against the extemperoneous engineering of tumultuary assailants; and I doubt if Todleben[1] himself could have suggested a more scientific or more effectual way than we employed, of securing it, by works easily thrown up, against nocturnal aggression. Watch and ward were also kept; till morning dawned on our untried defences and nodding sentinels.

Whatever had been the feelings of the provinces, certainly Rome gave no proof of sympathy with revolution, but rather manifested enthusiastic devotion to her new sovereign. Upon the Civic Guard being enlarged, to enable regular troops to move northward, multitudes presented themselves for enrolment; and among these, persons of the highest class, eager to take on themselves the defence of the Pope's sacred person. Prince Altieri* received command of this body. The loyalty of the poorer classes became almost alarming. They surrounded the royal carriage in such masses, that it was scarcely possible to move through them; and they expressed their attachment and readiness to fight, with a clamour and a warmth that would have rendered any attempt to remove them a dangerous experiment.

The Pope displayed the utmost calmness, fortitude, and

---

1. Eduard Ivanovich Todleben (1818-84). Russian general of German origin famous for his ingenious defensive engineering strategies.

prudence. The blow was, no doubt, to him cruel and disappointing. It served better than any symbolical ceremony, to remind him, on his coronation day, how earthly glory passeth quickly away. He was yet untried, determined to devote himself to his high duties with zeal and ability. He had every reason to hope that he should continue the peaceful career of his predecessors. There was no army worth naming kept up in the States—one burthen the less, to press on the people. Repression had never been a contemplated principle of government; military occupation had not been considered as the tenure of an ecclesiastical dynasty. There was one consolation certainly in what had just occurred. The insurrection had broken out before his election was known. It could have no personal motive, no enmity to himself. It arose against the rule, not against the ruler; against the throne, not against the actual possessor.

Neither could it be said that the revolution was a last measure, after preliminary efforts,—the resources of men driven to extremity, by being denied all redress. The outburts was sudden, though doubtless premeditated; it aimed at the final overthrow of the reigning power, not modifications of government. It pretended to seek, not reforms, but the substitution of a republic for the existing and recognised rule. Now let anyone impartially discuss with himself, what he would have done in similar circumstances; and it will be difficult for him to arrive at condemnation of the course pursued by Gregory. There was no question of concession, but of cession only. His governors and representatives had been driven away, and an army was forcing its way towards his capital, not to make terms with him, but to expel him. They were prepared to treat with him, not as aggrieved subjects, but as the supreme rulers. They were now the nation, the government; sitting in provisional form, in provincial cities, distracted, unorganised. Was it his duty to recognise at once their claims; and, if they proved unable to drive him from Rome, to divide his States with them, and surrender, at the bidding of at most a faction, the rich provinces over

GREGORY THE SIXTEENTH

which he had just been appointed? Or was he to yield to this violence, because, in the confidence of a paternal rule, the papacy had not kept up a disproportionate standing army during peace?

If not; if any one similarly circumstanced would have felt that his first duty was to secure integral possession of his rightful dominions, and to rescue the country from civil war; there was no alternative but the one adopted by Gregory; the calling in the aid of an allied power, especially one to whom the well-known lesson applied—

"Nam tua res agitur, paries cum proximus ardet."[1]

That foreign assistance,[2] especially when prolonged, is an evil, no one can doubt; and as such none more deplored it than Gregory XVI. But there was only a choice of evils; and surely this one was less than anarchy and all its miseries. In fact, it is a mistake to speak of choice; since it was a necessity without alternative. For the outbreak itself, independent of all abstract questions, was a grievous calamity to the country. Its promoters, of course, appropriated to themselves the provincial chests, and cut off supplies from the capital, where public payments had to be made; the additional expenses entailed by it, and the irregularities that ensued in the collection of revenues, embarassed for a long time the public finances: a loan had to be contracted for the first time, and an external debt created; public property had to be ruinously sold, and profitable sources of national income farmed out for a present advantage and eventual loss; and much property belonging to ecclesiastical corporations was enfranchised and its proceeds converted into Government funds. But in the meantime payments of all sorts ran into

1. Quintus Flaccus Horace: Epistle 1.18.84. [One's own affairs are at stake when the wall next door is burning.]
2. The Austrian government sent in troops to aid the Pope; they finally left in July 1831. The French Government had tried to prevent Austrian assistance, but Metternich ignored their representations.

arrears, whether dividends, salaries, pensions, or assignments; and I can speak with painful recollection of the embarassment in which persons charged with administration of property vested in public securities soon found themselves involved, through the disturbance created by this internal derangement. It was several years before the financial current again flowed regularly and smoothly.

In the mean time the Pope was not merely calm and confident, but most active; and no one, reading the public acts of the first year of Pontificate, would imagine that it was one of intestine war, confusion and distress. Within the month of his nomination (February 28) he preconised, as it is called, twenty-two archbishops and bishops; in the September following he published seventeen more, and twelve cardinals, several of them men of considerable merit.

In March he ordered the magnificent tunnels for the Anio at Tivoli to be commenced. He reduced the duties on salt and flour, and modified other imports; created chambers of commerce in various cities, including the metropolis; issued excellent laws for municipal government, and reorganised that for several provinces, raising their rank for their advantage; introduced great improvements in the Code of Procedure, criminal and civil; and established a sinking fund for the gradual extension of the newly-contracted debt.

But perhaps the most striking act of the first year of pressure and revolt was the publication of an Apostolic Constitution, which was dated August 31, beginning "*Solicitudo Ecclesiarum.*" It was mentioned that Cardinal Cappellari had been the chief instrument in granting bishops to the infant republics of South America; in fact it was he whom Leo XII had deputed in 1827 to treat with Labrador, the envoy sent by Ferdinand VII to Rome, expressly to oppose this concession. Labrador was acknowledged by all parties, and especially by the diplomatic body in Rome, to be one of the most accomplished and most able statesmen in Europe, yet he could not carry his point.

The sentiment maintained by Cardinal Cappellari as a negotiator were authoritively proclaimed by him as Pope in the Bull just mentioned; that the Holy See recognises governments established *de facto*, without thereby going into the question of abstract rights. At the moment when changes were rapidly made in governments and dynasties, and when sceptres passed from hand to hand with the rapidity of magical and illusory exhibitions, it was at once bold and prudent to lay down simple principles by which the judgment of the Holy See might be easily anticipated; while it kept itself clear of all internal disputes and embarassing appeals during actual contests.

CHAPTER II

PUBLIC WORKS OF GREGORY THE SIXTEENTH

THE recollections in the first volume[1] commenced in the nineteenth year of one Pontificate; but it was almost necessary to carry back the reader to eventful occurrences preceding the period of personal remembrance. They reach their term four years before the close of this fourth reign; but, in a similar manner, I must be allowed to refer to circumstance that followed my separation from the scene of youth and manhood.

However warlike may appear the attitude, which Gregory was compelled to assume at the commencement of his reign, the arts which stamped it with their character were the arts of peace. Scarcely any Pontificate has its foot-prints more deeply or more widely impressed on it than his. He was not content with continuing or extending what his predecessors had commenced, but he created; that is, beginning from nothing, and accomplished what, until his time, was altogether wanting.

1. *Pius VII*, Fisher Press, 2003.

Nor did he confine himself to any one department of art; his attention was comprehensive and generous, not guided by caprice, but directed by a discerning taste.

Let us begin with these higher proofs of genius. The Roman galleries were rich till his time in masterpieces of Greek and Roman art. Indeed one only wonders how so much that is beautiful remains there after Rome has enriched the rest of the world. Unfortunately, in ancient times, many of the sculptures which were excavated when the soil was from the first time upturned, were placed in the palaces and villas belonging to the family of the reigning Pope, and thereby became appropriated to its own use. Thus, the Medici Villa received those matchless statues and groups which make the Tribuna at Florence a temple of highest art, though adorned only with spoils secretly conveyed from Rome. Thus also, whatever in the Museum of Naples bears the name of Farnesian, as the Hercules and Dirce, came from the gigantic palace of that family in Rome. Let us imagine these two collections poured back into their original source, and what would the Vatican be now? Then add to the sum of Roman artistic wealth the innumerable pieces of sculpture collected or scattered in other places, and even in other parts of the city; in the villas and palaces of Rome, in the Louvre, at Munich, in London, and it may well be said that the Eternal City has not only heaped up artistic treasures for herself, but has enriched with them the entire world.

With this inexhaustible mine of wealth, she had not thought of going beyond her own soil to increase her store. She watches indeed more jealously over it, and over every new discovery, and does not allow the stranger, so easily as formerly, to be a gainer by her losses. The consequence has been most beneficial. Unable any longer to look to Italy for the accumulation of masterpieces, we have turned to the original fields where she reaped her golden harvest, to Greece and Asia, to Lycia and Halicarnassus. It was Gregory XVI who first enlarged the boundaries of artistic

GREGORY THE SIXTEENTH 15

collection in Rome, and brought into near connection the monuments of earlier schools, those from which it had always been supposed that the more elegant and sublime productions of Grecian taste and genius had received their first inspirations.

The discovery of Assyrian monuments has indeed materially modified these theories. Egypt can no longer claim to be the cradle of artistic Greece; no lawgiver of her future code of taste ever lurked in the bulrushes of the Nile. And Etruscan art is no antecedent preparer or modifier of Grecian grace; it is a portion of it, finished and refined, though corresponding with it in progressive development, from rigid archaism to unzoned luxuriancy.

Gregory added to the Vatican—but kept unblended with its chaster treasures—most valuable collections of these two classes of monuments. He began nearest home. Mention has already been made of the Etruscan discoveries commenced a few years earlier in the Papal territory.[1] Campania had long supplied Europe with what are still called Etruscan vases, probably the same objects of commerce as figure in our customs list under the designation of "Magna Græcia ware." The museum of Naples was rich in its collections of them; and most other countries possessed a few specimens. North of Rome, most Etrurian cities contained local museums, in which were deposited curiosities, as they are called, picked up in the neighbourhood. Chiusi, Volterra, Cortona, and other successors of old Etruscan towns, treasured up with care the remains and evidences of their ancient taste and splendour. Sometimes an antiquarian academy or society occupied itself with researches and discussions on the spot, and published learned and useful *Transactions*. Such are those of the Academia of Cortona, which extend to many volumes, full of interesting matter.

But a few years before the accession of Gregory, a rich vein of excavation had been struck into, situated beyond the

1. *Leo XII and Pius VIII*, Fisher Press, 2005, p. 35.

confines of modern Tuscany, but within the territory of ancient Etruria. The very names of Vulci, Tarquinii, and Cerae suggest to classical ears the idea of places belonging to that ancient confederation; but the names had themselves been buried like the cities to which they belonged, under such designations as Arco della Badia, Ponte d'Asso, or Cannino. In the last of these places, the Prince who takes his title from it, Lucien Bonaparte, made extensive researches, and drew from them an immense collection, which has found its way to the British Museum. Etruscan 'diggings' became the rage; and many adventurers were amply repaid.

It was not the ruins of cities that were sought, but their cemeteries. The custom of savage nations, so often prolonged into high civilisation, of providing the dead with the implements and furniture which they needed on earth, to serve them in an ideal world,—that usage which suggested the slaughter of the soldier's war steed, or of the sovereign's wife, and the burying of his army with the first, or the putting the luck penny into the hand of the rich or poor, to pay his freightage to the churlish ferryman;[1] was fully appreciated and observed by the old Italians. The tomb of a respectable person occupied the space of a cottage; its walls were painted with frescoes of banquets, games, horses, and men in large dimensions; and within was exquisite furniture in imperishable bronze, seats, beds, lamps, and other household utensils, of the same metal, or of more fragile but more richly laboured clay. Nor were vases there most precious contents; but gold and jewelled ornaments, entombed there in profusion, attest the wealth, the luxury, and taste of ancient races,[2] as well as their reverence for their dead. Breast-plates elaborately wrought of purest gold, neck-laces, ear-rings, bullas for children's necks, chains of elaborate patterns, all exquisitely wrought, and

1. Charon, in Greek myths, ferried the dead across the Styx to Hades.
2. The East is full of fables concerning vast treasures, yet concealed in the sepulchres of monarchs, guarded by griffins or spirits. The account of David's tomb, in connection with Herod, has become a matter of history.

enriched with pearls and gems, were found even in abundance, and many yet serve as models for the goldsmith's art.

A glut in the market became an almost unavoidable result of this superabundance of discovery. The Government of Rome, being on the spot, had the advantage of choice; and Gregory XVI, with unbounded liberality, purchased all that could be required to form, at once, a complete collection. There was already in the Vatican library, a most choice selection of vases; a celebrated real chariot was in the museum; other beautiful statues in bronze, one with an inscription on the arm, were scattered about. These were brought together in a suite of ample halls, which formerly were the Cardinal Librarian's apartment, but had not been occupied for many years.

It belongs to the 'Hand-books' and 'Guides' to give a description of this splendid collection, and its admirable arrangements. Suffice it to say, that nothing seems to have been overlooked. There is one model of a tomb, with its furniture as it was found; and there are traced copies of the frescoes, many of which fell to dust soon after contact with the air. The wonder is, how they had remained so many ages beyond its reach. That families should not have assumed that they had made rather a loan than a gift of their treasures to the dead, and after a decent interval of mourning, have resumed possession; that domestics should not have filched them, or a fraternity of jewel—if not body-snatchers—should not have existed for sepulchral burglaries; that in the feuds between tribes, when cities were given to sack and ruin, rings snatched from the ears of matrons, and embroidered baldricks stripped from the bodies of slaughtered warriors, the ashes of the dead should have afforded protection to gold and pearl[1] more efficaceously than horses and chariots; and finally, that during the ages of Roman dominion, when the traditions of older

1. See Flavius Josephus*, *Early History of the Jews*, tom. i. pp. 412 & 802, ed. Havercamp*. In the second passage we are told that Herod found, not money, as Hyrcanus* had, but "many gold ornaments and precious things."

sepulchral rites were still preserved, or in the medieval period, when no fable of guardian dragons terrified marauders from the plunder of Pagan graves, these mounds, visible to every eye, should have sealed up their treasures and kept them faithfully, till a better motive and a more intelligent spirit kindly transferred them to a surer custody and to admiring observation, may be truly considered one of those secondary dispensations of Providence, which make the works of man's hands, thus buried for ages, able to fructify in the social world; like the seed-corn found in Egyptian sepulchres, which has, after thousands of years, germinated and given harvests.

It was on the anniversary of his election, February the 2nd, 1837, that Gregory opened his Etruscan museum; two anniversaries later he inaugurated its fellow-collection, the Egyptian. It occupies the floor immediately below the first.

In one way, Rome may be said to have anticipated all other countries in gathering Egyptian monuments, and in making them known to Europe, before the collections of Drovetti* and Belzoni* enriched it, and in exhibiting such a class of them as no other city can hope to rival.

For centuries the obelisks of Rome, prostrate or standing, had been almost the only specimens of Egytpian art known to scholars and to artists. They are now seven of eight in number, one having been erected by Pius VI on the Quirinal, one in my time on the Pincian by his successor. But the ones before the Vatican and the Lateran, the first plain, and the second richly storied, had long been objects of admiration to every traveller. Their gigantic dimensions and elegant forms, their unimaginable material and finished workmanship, whether in polish or in carving; then their preserved integrity as monoliths for so many thousands of years, and the calculations of the mechanical strength and skill which were required to extract them from their granite beds,—transport them and raise them on to proportional pedestals— a piling of Pelion on Ossa,—had, perhaps more practically than anything else, given the West a notion of

GREGORY THE SIXTEENTH

the precocious civilisation and huge works which so early distinguished the banks of the Nile. And, except by the one importation of a second-class obelisk to Paris under Louis-Philippe, there has been no attempt to invade this monopoly of the Eternal City.

Besides this singular order of monuments which cannot be brought into a collection, there were other primitive Egyptian pieces of sculpture, scattered through Rome, the full value of which was not ascertained till the discovery of the Egyptian alphabet by Young[1] and Chapollion*. Such, for instance, were two of the four basalt lions, which, couched at the feet of Moses, delivered well-regulated jets of water from their indrawn lips into the fountain bearing that patriarch's name. They were covered with hieroglyphics, which, read by the learned F. Ungarelli,[2] showed them to belong to a very early dynasty, and to be perhaps coeval with the Jewish lawgiver himself.

These and any other such remains were replaced by less noble substitutes in their servile occupations, and received a place in the halls of the Vatican amidst other kingly monuments. But there was a third class of Egyptian, or rather pseudo-Egyptian works, which likewise belonged exclusively to Rome. The emperor Adrian[3] collected in his villa at Tivoli imitations of celebrated buildings in every part of the world. Among the rest was a "Canopus,"[4] adorned by Egyptian works, or rather Greco-Roman sculptures reduced to Egyptian forms. The museums abounded with such monuments drawn from the ruins of the villa; and these also were withdrawn from their usurped positions, and united to their more legitimate brethren; thus producing a contrast between the white marble progeny of

1. Dr. Thomas Young (1774-1829). Physician, who also published work on decyphering Egyptian hieroglyphics. Born in Somerset and educated at Göttingen and Edinburgh; he was inspired by Belzoni's discoveries in Egypt.
2. F. Ungarelli. Barnabite priest, Egyptologist, and friend of Champollion.
3. Hadrian (117-138AD) built the largest and richest of the Imperial villa complexes at Tivoli between 125 and 134 A.D.   4. Egyptian jar.

Western, and the dusky granite and basalt productions of Eastern art.

Pius VII had purchased a small but valuable collection brought from Egypt by Signor Guidi, and had placed it round a hemicycle in the Vatican, that crossed the end of the great Belvedere court, uniting its two flanks. It could only be considered as placed there temporarily, and it migrated to the new quarters prepared for Ises and Anabises, Cynocephali and Scarabæi.

Such was the groundwork of this new aggregation to the vast Vatican group of artistic wonders; it need not be added, that every opportunity has been embraced of increasing and perfecting the work so happily commenced. Nor can it be necessary to observe that the decoration of this, as of every other department of art-collection, is strictly in keeping with its particular object,—and is here purely Egyptian, as elsewhere Etruscan or Grecian.

The Gallery of paintings in the Vatican can hardly be designated by that name, which suggests the idea of walls covered with pictures from ceiling to wainscot, whether stretched into great lengths as in Paris or Florence, or surrounding halls as in London and Dresden. In all other collections quantity gives value, to a certain extent; and a sufficient exemplification of every celebrated schools is kept in view. They are all galleries for study.

At the Vatican, however, this is not the case. A few paintings, chiefly large, are hung without crowding one another, or unfairly contrasting, on ample spaces of wall, in lofty, spacious apartments, three or four being indulged in the room which would elsewhere suffice for fifty or a hundred tightly fitting frames. It was not easy to place them well; and accordingly I can remember at least four situations in the immense Vatican where they have been uncomfortably situated. Gregory, in 1836, bestowed on them their present position, in which they will probably be visited for generations to come. One of the first places which they occupied was the "*Appartamento Borgia*," a series of ten

GREGORY THE SIXTEENTH

noble halls at the palace end of the Belvedere court, painted most beautifully in their ceilings by some Pre-Raffaelite artists. Gregory XVI added this range to the already vast library, and filled it with additional books.

Another department of the literary treasure he particularly treasured is its Christian museum. To this he made splendid additions at his own expense; among other ways, by bestowing on it a most rare and valuable series of early Byzantine paintings, in beautiful preservation. He likewise purchased for himself, and left in the palace, the whole collection of pictures by Peters, an eminent German animal painter,[1] and a man of genuine worth and simplest mind, who died at an advanced age in Rome.

It would be unfair to consider the detached paintings hung against walls as composing exclusively the Vatican gallery. One must comprehend under this title the Sixtine Chapel as the grandest specimen of Michelangelo's masterly genius; the *Stanze* and *Loggie* as the noblest display of Raphael's sweetest powers; St Lawrence's Chapel as a gem without flaw of Beato Angelico's work, set in the very centre of Raffael's golden band; not to speak of twenty other great artists, before and since, who have left noble works upon the vaults and walls of that grandest of palaces.

It was Gregory XVI who thought of arresting the progress of decay in some valuable portions of these sublime works. So little consciousness was there of their inimitable powers in the greatest artists, that they did not think of sheltering their works from the most inevitable causes of destruction; they painted in the open portico, where rain and sun would play alternately; as if they took it for granted that whatever they did must of course perish, and be replaced by other men as gifted as themselves.

It has always been the same. What Greek sculptor

1. Probably Herman Peters. Wiseman claimed possession of the only picture of a human being that he ever painted. He says that Herman's large picture of Paradise included Adam and Eve, but they were very small in size, and the animals were clearly the principal objects of his attention.

expected his marble—brittle to the touch of any boy's pebble, defaceable under long exposure to the elements—to be placed within the shelter, and not as soon be erected on the roof of a temple? So when too late, the frescoes of Raffael, and the arabesques and stuccoes of his pupils, were found to have been almost lost,—indeed, preserved only by early copies and engravings, Gregory, however, continued the work of preservation, before and since carried on, of enclosing the whole *Loggie* with glass, after having had the frescoes of the upper corridor admirably restored by Professor Agricola*.

It was natural to expect that, however vast the Vatican might be, it would not suffice for the unceasing impouring of new museums, as well as of individual objects of artistic merit. It had overflowed already; and Gregory had made its very gardens precious by the multitude of statues, vases, and altars with which he had embellished them; for he may be said to have entirely renewed them, or even to have laid them out afresh.

It was found necessary to devote some other large building to the purpose of containing works which the Vatican and Capitol either could not contain, or could not suitably harbour; for new discoveries or acquisitions had been made of statues and other works that deserved conspicuous places, and would not brook collocation among inferior productions.

Such was the beautiful Antinous, purchased from the Braschi Palace, rescued from Russian possession by the right of preëmption reserved to the Government: and the sublime Sophocles, the rival or equal of the Naples Aristides, discovered and given to the Pope in 1830 by the family of the present Antonelli*.

But what perhaps primarily demanded extensive accomodation was an immense mosaic pavement representing worthies of the *cestus* (the boxer's glove), eminent boxers and wrestlers in their day, natives of Tuscan cities, which were proud, one may suppose, of their sons' thews and sinews. These heroes of the ring have been suddenly restored to fame, and are likely to obtain a second immortality, if one may use the phrase, more enduring than the first. Their proportions are colossal, as they stand full-lengths in separate compartments; it required no restricted space to stretch them forth in their original position.

The Lateran Palace, a noble pile, had long stood untenanted, except for a time, as a receptacle for paupers. The Treasurer, Monsignor Tosti*, had thoroughly repaired it, and restored it to its primeval beauty; yet it was insuffient and ill-suited for a Papal residence. The Ædes Lateranae,—confiscated under Nero, celebrated by poets and historians as most sumptious, given by Maxentius to Constantine as his daughter's dowry, and by Constantine, with its adjoining basilica, to be the episcopal palace and cathedral of Christian Rome,—were admirably adapted for the purpose of a new, not merely supplementary museum.

The first evidence of fitness was, that the huge *Palæstrae* mosaic carpeted one of its halls, as if it had been bespoken for the purpose of some ancient tessellator. And so were separate shrines found there for masterpieces, and galleries or chambers for lesser works, one of which is a copy in mosaic of a celebrated floor-painting, described by Pliny as existing at Pergamum, and representing an 'unswept pavement' after supper. Gregory XVI was the founder of this new museum, which under the present Pope has received not only greater development, but in some respects a distinct destination, as a depository of Christian sculptures.

CHAPTER III

EVENTS OF GREGORY'S PONTIFICATE

EVERY state or government presents two distinct aspects and conditions, one internal, another external. In this it is like any other association, any family, any individual. We know little or nothing of what is going on within the circle of persons next door to us,—of the struggles, or jars, or privations, or illnesses, or afflictions; or of the domestic joys, affections, and pleasures inside any house but our own. There is a hidden life too in every separate being that composes each humble circle, impenetrable to the rest of its members. No one can read the mind, block out the desires, trace the intentions of others with whom he has lived for years in contact. Hence he must needs be content to act with them according to the form in which they show themselves, and in proportion that we require one another's coöperation.

Is it not so with kingdoms and principalities? What do we know of the internal policy, the yearly growth, the daily actions of rulers and people, in states especially that have not attained an influential prominence? Fot the readers of newspapers, volumes are daily prepared of home-stirring information, to be eagerly devoured: how much of it will have an interest beyond the hawser's length that moors the Dover packet?

Who will care in France or Germany what illustrious guests the Sovereign entertained sumptiously yesterday at her table; or who spoke at the last Bradford or Wolverhampton Reform meeting? Their very names defy spelling or pronunciation beyond the channel. And so, how little do we inquire what is going on, for example, in Hesse-Homburg of Reuss; or who troubled himself about 'the

Principalities, or their internal affairs, till their outward life came into close contact with those of other governments? As a matter of course, it is impossible for those who are absorbed in their own interests, and fully occupied with their own internal concerns, to penetrate into the real feelings, or invest themselves with the circumstances, that belong to another nation, perhaps even a different race.

Like any other country, Rome has its twofold existence. Of its exterior action, of the part which it openly takes in European politics, of its treaties, its tariffs, its commerce, of course everyone may judge, and has probably data on which to attempt at least to judge. But it is more than probable that the real condition of the country, the character of its laws, the sentiments of the mass of the prople, will be no better known than are those of other states, beyond the interior sphere which they affect. No one can for a moment believe that the occasional, and too evidently partisan, communication to a newspaper constitutes the materials upon which an accurate judgment can be formed; while no trouble is taken to the statistical, financial, moral or social state of the country, the administration of the state, or the inward changes gradually introduced.

Yet, while such indifference is manifested concerning the interior state of other sovereignties, no such reserve is permitted about Rome; and it seems to be imagined that it is within everyone's power to discover evils there; and to prescribe their remedy. There surely is a very different reason for this interest than ordinary philanthropy; nor does it need to be defined.

Let us take Rome for what it is, a State recognised by all Europe, as governed, for high and important reasons, by an ecclesiastical Ruler; and further assuming that he is no more to be expected than any other head of a realm to commit suicidal acts against himself or his authority, nor to yield to desires or attempts of those who plan and desire the overthrow of both; we may then surely consider him a good sovereign who devotes the whole of his mind and energies to the happiness of his subjects, endeavouring to effect improvements in every department of state and in every part of his dominions. Now, certainly, no monarch ever did more conscientiously labour, body and soul, for the good of those committed to him, and for the discharge of his public duties, than the virtuous Gregory XVI.

It has been mentioned, that, in the very year of his accession, he published new laws on the course of judicial procedure. In the following year he issued another decree on crimes and punishments. In 1833 he reorganised the Secretary of State's office, dividing it into two departments, of Home and Foreign Affairs; and further gave a new system to the Department of Works.

In 1834 a national bank was established for the first time in Rome; and a complete code was published of laws and regulations for all public administration. The year following, a new coinage was issued more perfectly reduced to the decimal system than before; as the gold coins previously bore no proportion to it. The entire Roman Forum was thoroughly restored; and the monastery of St Gregory, a conspicuous public edifice, with the space and road around it, was repaired and beautified at the Pope's own expense.

Very large public works were also executed at the mouth of the Tiber, and in the harbour and city of Città Vecchia. The Anio also was sent this year through its two new tunnels; and finally a cemetery which had been commenced outside the walls, at the basilica of St Lawrence, was finished and opened; burying in it being made compulsory, and intramural sepulture being suppressed. In 1836 night schools were first established.

The year 1837 was a dark one in the annals of Gregory's pontificate. The cholera had visited several parts of the States, and had been particularly severe in Ancona. The Pope succoured liberally from his own funds, as well as from public sources, every place which was attacked; but, at the same time, he omitted no precautionary measures in his capital. It would be superfluous to say that every religious act of expiation was duly performed. There were sermons in many churches, exhorting the people to repentance, that so the Divine wrath might be appeased, and the scourge averted. There was a solemn procession, in which the Holy Father walked.

But some questioned the prudence of thus asembling crowds together; and the events seem partly to justify them. A sanitary commission was formed, towards which the Pope largely subscribed. Supernumerary hospitals were sought: the English College was unreservedly offered to the authorities, with the services of its inmates to attend the sick. The building was surveyed, and accepted as an hospital for convalescents; but this did not require any help from the students, who, being obliged to leave the house, retired to their Tusculan villa.

There we were regularly in a state of siege. Every town and village exercised its municipal rights to the utmost, and surrounded itself with a sanitary cordon, which was as jeolous of foreign approach as the dragon guardian of the Hesperides. Hence all communication between neighbouring hamlets was cut off, and it was only by stealth that the capital itself could be visited.

In our own village[1] we organised a committee of health composed of natives and of English; every room in every house was visited, cleaned and whitewashed where needful; every nuisance abated; wholesome provisions furnished to all in need; and, as medical attendance is at public charge in all Roman communes,[2] we supplied medicines at free cost. Thus we kept our dear village of Monte Porzio healthy and cheerful, while within-doors we provided ample means of recreation for ourselves and the more intelligent inhabitants.

1. Monte Porzio.
2. The existence of free medical care in the Papal States at this time may come as a surprise to those who regard the British National Health Service as a pioneer of free medicine and treatment in the nineteen forties.

The Pope remained at his post in Rome, attending to everything, bestowing larger alms, and providing for every want. Thus at length the scourge passed by, and the avenging angel sheathed his sword, after raising the mortality of the twelvemonth (between Easter and Easter) from three to twelve thousand deaths.

New duties then arose. The Holy Father put himself at the head of the subscriptions for educating the numerous orphans left destitute by the plague. Charity here was universal. The English College, like many other institutions, undertook the support of two children. Houses were opened, by charitable contributions, for those who remained; and among the most active and conspicuous agents in this merciful work was our countrywoman the Princess Borghese*, the Lady Gwendoline Talbot, daughter of the Earl of Shrewsbury; a rarely gifted lady, whose memory yet lives in Rome in the prayers of the poor and the admiration of the great. It may be added that the statistics of the cholera have nowhere been compiled with greater accuracy and minuteness than in Rome.

In spite of these anxious cares, this year saw its important improvements. Besides the opening of the Etruscan museum, and the enlargement of the Christian collection, both already mentioned, and the complete restoration of the Pauline Chapel in the Vatican, there was established, for the first time in the Roman States, a general insurance company, embracing insurance against hail as well as fire.

The year 1838 was remarkable for one of the most interesting antiquarian discoveries of modern times. The gate known as the Porta Maggiore, from its vicinity to the church of Santa Maria Maggiore, passes under a magnificent point of union of several aqueducts, adorned with splendid inscriptions. But the gate had been fortified by most barbaric work in the middle ages. These hideous appendages were ordered to be removed, and the consequence was, not only the unveiling of the fine old work above the gate, but the unburying of a monument singular in its construction and in its mystery. An excrescent bastion at the outside of the gate was subjected to excision, and disclosed in the process that its core was an ancient tomb, of republican times, built with strange materials. It had been raised by Marcus Vergilius Eurysaces to his nameless wife; and, as he was a rich baker, for he was a public contractor (*redemptor*), he called the tomb a bakery (*pistrinum*), and built up its walls of stone kneading troughs, surmounted by reliefs, which represent the whole process of making bread.

Another curious appearance no less astonished Rome,— this was the arrival of two Ottoman ambassadors; the first, Ahmed Fethis Pasha, on his was to Paris; the second, one since more renowned, Redschid Pasha, minister of Mahmoud II in London, who came to thank the Pope for his kindness to his colleague. I remember a saying of one of these intelligent Turks, when he was shown the Pantheon, and told what it formerly was, "Where" he asked, "are the statues of the heathen gods?" "Of course they were removed when the temple was christianised," was the natural answer. "No," he replied; "I would have left them standing to show how the true God had triumphed over them in their own house."

It was in this year also that the Vatican library received the addition of ten rooms. Besides many great public works, some already mentioned, the year 1839 was signalled by the publication of a remarkable document, the Bull "*In supremo apostolatus fastigio*" (December 8), against the slave trade. There can be no doubt that in several countries this splendid decree did more to put down the slave-trade than negotiations or corvettes. Of this I was assured by several natives of those countries. It contains a most interesting account, by way of recital, of the untiring activity of former popes to put an end to the infamous traffic.[1]

This year witnessed perhaps the most splendid function

---

1. Thus St Wolstan's preaching prevailed more for the same purpose with the Bristol merchants than royal prohibitions.

which the Church ever performs, the canonisation of five saints. Many years of severe investigations and judicial processes are required to prepare for this final and solemn recognition of sublime holiness in any of God's chosen servants. Only a few times in a century—twice, so far, in this—does it fall to the lot of a Pontiff to perform it.

The entire basilica of St Peter is superbly decorated and brilliantly illuminated; paintings of great events in the lives of the glorified person adorn it in every part. All the bishops of the Papal States, and many from other parts of Italy, and even from more distant countries, usually attend. These are united in one magnificent procession: and on this occasion I remember one venerable grey-headed man who supported the pendant of St Alphonsus Liguori's* banner; he was the saint's nephew, and had been confirmed by him.

The following year, 1840, closes all personal recollections of this excellent Pontiff, except during a short visit of a few weeks two years later. For in this year it was thought advisable to increase the number of bishops in England, by subdividing the four apostolic vicariates established in the reign of James II, so as to double their number. In fact this had been a matter of absolute necessity. For example, the northern vicariate comprised not only the four counties usually designated by that epithet, but Lancashire and Yorkshire besides.

Since this first distribution of episcopal jurisdiction, cities and towns, like Manchester, Liverpool, Leeds and Newcastle, had arisen from secondary rank to the dimension of capitals; without mentioning innumerable other manufacturing places, or rather districts, composed of clusters, or chains formed by busy seats of industry, with a growing population.

Four new bishops were accordingly named; and in additon to these, the writer was appointed to the subordinate situation of coadjutor or assistant to one already in possession of a see with residence in Wolverhampton,

GREGORY THE SIXTEENTH

the venerable Bishop Walsh. It was a sorrowful evening, at the beginning of autumn, when, after residence in Rome prolonged through twenty-two years, till affection clung to every old stone there, like the moss that grew into it, this strong but tender tie was cut, and much of future happiness had to be invested in the mournful recollections of the past.

> *Cum subit illius tristissimus noctis imago,*
> *Quae mihi supremum tempus in urbe fuit,*
> *Cum repeto noctem qua tot mihi chara reliqui.*
> *Labitur ex oculis nunc quoque gutta meis.*[1]

In the chronological sketch here given only a few occurrences of each year have been selected: sufficient to show how intent Gregory XVI was upon steady improvement. It would be easy to multiply examples even of material progress under his pontificate. The first steamers that struggled against the chafed and eddying Tiber made their appearance during it; and though in his old age he would not embark in the still slowly progressing undertaking of railways, he always said that his successor must perforce involve himself in their more rapid extension.

For those in one country, whose improvements naturally take a given direction, to scorn others becasue they follopw another direction equally congenial to them, and in which they may in their turn give the lead to the scoffers, is surely narrow and ungenerous. With boundless resources and infinite advantages, England has her definite career of progress, and in it may leave every other country far behind. On the other hand, it is but lately that she has awakened to her own

---

1. Ovid (Publius Ovidius Naso). *Tristia*, Bk. 1, III, 1-4. [When I come under siege from poignant memories of that night which marked my last moments in the city, and I go back over a night in which I abandoned many things that were dear to me, even now some drops of tears slip from my eyes.]

deficiencies in whatever relates to the beautiful arts. Italy gladly yields the palm to her in all industrial pursuits; admires, studies, and strives, with far more limited means, sometimes too subserviently, to copy.

But it does not jeer her, in return, for her backwardness in just becoming conscious of her artistic imperfection, nor for her somewhat awkward ways of seeking to repair it. Let there be, not so much forbearance as mutual commendation, meted out by the equitable standard of effort rather than of success. For the first is the measure of the will, the second of the power; the one belongs to man, the other more strictly to Providence. That may be of instantaneous formation and of immediate growth, this may require or may have required centuries to mature. The former can be equal in many, the latter is of necessity unequally distributed. On these just principles, it will be found that much more has been done by peaceful and gradual advance than could have been effected by the fitful and violent shocks of revolutionary propulsions.

CHAPTER IV

SOME OF THE REMARKABLE MEN OF GREGORY THE SIXTEENTH'S PONTIFICATE

DURING so long a reign as that of Gregory it might naturally be expected that some persons of more than usual distinction would adorn his court and city; for it has been the time-respected privilege of both to attract from without, as well as to nurture at home, men of genius, learning, and singular virtue.

Two remarkable instances may be given of this attractive power; the one connected with, the other independent of, religion; yet both exhibited in the same race. While it must be confessed that the native school of painting has clung unreasonably as yet to the classical style, and sought its subjects in heathen mythology as most exuberantly lending itself to the luxuries of art, there has, nevertheless, lived for a long period in the midst of it a school of foreign Christian painting, born and bred in Rome itself. Nay, we may even say that the entire religious art of modern Germany, not excluding Düsseldorf itself, owes its happy birth to that nursery of every art.

Many years ago, several young German artists—would that they were still young!—associated themselves in Rome to draw and paint, taking for their models the purer and sweeter types of earlier periods, when religion walked hand in hand with the three great sisters, whose badges are the pencil, the chisel, and the compass; or rather when they followed her as willing handmaids.

While yet comparatively unknown, they executed a joint, yet separate, work, by painting in fresco, as in old times, vaults and walls, with their accessories, in three halls in the Massimo Villa at the Lateran. Each took one apartment, and with it, one division of Dante's golden art-poem; so that the Inferno, Purgatorio, and Paradiso, furnished the exclusive theme of each contribution. To this day the works retain their freshness, and may well rank among the most beautiful of modern performances, though little seen and known to travellers.

Of this generous trio, so intrepid in breaking through modern feeling in art, only one settled, and has reached his maturity in Rome—the honoured and venerated Overbeck*, Cornelius* was another, who has left indelible proofs of his genius at Münich and Berlin. Veith*, I think, was the third, the father too of a Christian school at Frankfurt.

In Rome, Overbeck's influence has been ever beneficial, especially among his own countrymen. There is a fraternity of German artists in Rome, who devote themselves to Christian painting; and one is glad to say, receive much, if not most, of their encouragement from English patrons.

And in Germany it will be found that every local school of similar principles springs from a master who, directly or indirectly, has been formed in Rome. The venerable Baron von Schadow*, President of the eminently religious school of Düsseldorf, as well as his brother,* a distinguished sculptor, was for some years an inhabitant of that city.

Side by side was another purely scientific association, composed of Germans, and havings its seat on the Tarpeian Rock. It was first founded during the embassy of Chevalier Bunsen, and was under the auspices of the Prussian court and government, which subsidised it liberally. It held its meetings, and published its bulletins, or larger annual collections of essays, with valuable engravings, on every antiquarian topic.

If foreigners from beyond the Alps thus came spontaneously to Rome, to seek occupation for their genius or industry, we cannot be surprised if religion or ecclesiastical tastes brought many from other parts of Italy, as well as from abroad, to settle there for life.

Such, for instance, is the learned Father Theiner* of the Oratory, a Silesian by birth, now engaged in two gigantic works, each sufficient for the literary employment of one man at least; the continuation of Baronius'* *Ecclesiastical History*, and the complete collection of all documents relative to the Council of Trent. Yet he contrives, almost yearly, to bring out several volumes of inedited matter from the archives of the Vatican, over which he presides; making now that treasury of hidden documents as prolific as its super-incumbent library has been for years in the untiring hands of Cardinal Angelo Mai.

Another foreigner came to Rome in this Pontificate, of whom many readers will have heard, in one of what may be called two such extremes of life as seldom meet in one person. Those whose memory does not carry them back beyond the days of Waterloo may have found, in

Moore's politico-satirical poems,[1] mention of a person enjoying celebrity similar to that possessed more lately by a French Count resident in London; as a leader of fashion, remarkable at the same time for wit and accomplishments. Such was Baron Géramb, in the days "when George the Third was king."

But some may possibly remember a higher renown gained by him, beyond that of having his last *bon-mot* quoted in the morning papers. Being an alien, though neither a conspirator nor an assassin, he was ordered to leave the country, and refused. He barricaded his house, and placarded it with the words "Every Englishman's house is his castle," in huge letters. He bravely stood a siege of some duration, against the police of those days, and drew crowds around the house; till at length, whether starved out by a stern blockade, or overreached by a Bow-street strategy, he either yielded at discretion or was captured through want of it, and was forthwith transferred to a foreign shore.

So ends the first chapter of the public life of the gallant and elegant Baron Géramb, the charm of good society, to which by every title he belonged. What became of him after this? Did that society, on losing sight of him, ask any more? Probably few of those who had been entertained by his cleverness, or amused by his freaks, ever gave him another thought, and a commentator on Thomas Moore, encountering the "whiskers of Géramb" in one of his verses, might be at a loss to trace the history of their wearer. Certainly those ornaments of his countenance would have lent slight assistance in tracing him in after-life.

Many years later, in the reign of Gregory XVI, let the reader suppose himself to to be standing in the small plateau shaded by ilex, which fronts the Franciscan convent above Castel-Gandolfo. He is looking down on the lovely lake which takes its name from that village, through

1. Thomas Moore (1779-1852), Irish poet, satirist and man of letters.

an opening in the oaken screen, enjoying the breeze of an autumn afternoon. He may see, issuing from the convent-gate, a monk, not of its fraternity, but clothed in the white Cistercian habit; a man of portly dimensions, bestriding the humblest but most patriarchal of man-bearing animals, selected out of hundreds, his rider used to say, to be in just proportion to the burthen. If the stranger examines him, he will easily discern through the gravity of his look, not only a nobleness of countenance; and through the simplicity of his habit, not merely a gracefulness of demeanour, which speak the highly bred gentleman, but even visible remains of the good-humoured, kind-hearted, and soldierly courtier. There lurks still in his eye a sparkling gleam of wit suppressed, or disciplined into harmless coruscations. Once when I met him at Albano, he had brought as a gift to the English Cardinal Acton, a spirited sketch of himself and his "gallant grey" rolling together in the dust. When I called on him at his convent, he showed me an Imperial autograph letter, just received, announcing to him the gallantry and wounds of his son, fighting in Circassia, and several other royal epistles, written in the pleasant tone of friend to friend.

Yet he is thoroughly a monk of the strictest order known in the Church, living in a cell, without an object of luxury near him, sleeping on a straw pallet, occupied in writing, reading, meditating on holy things, devout in prayer, edifying in conversation. Among other works of his, overflowing with piety, is one peculiarly tender, entitled "My Saviour's Tomb." The good old monk had been to Jerusalem, and had manifested his affections by a novel and exquisite prodigality, borrowed in idea from a certain woman who had been a sinner in the city. He anointed the sepulchre of our Lord with the most costly of perfumes, the attergul, or otto of roses as we call it, so that the whole house was filled with its fragrance

Such is Père Géramb; such the second chapter of his known life. What had been the intermediate stage? When expelled, happily for him, from England, he very soon fell

GREGORY THE SIXTEENTH

into the enemy's hands, I know not how. But he happened to be cast into the same prison, I think Vincennes, where the good Cardinal De Gregorio* was also in bonds. He was first struck by the patience and virtues of his fellow captive, and gradually entered into conversation with him. The result was a change of heart and a change of life. Liberty soon put the sincerity of both to the test. Baron Géramb remained attached to the land of his captivity; in it he joined the fervent and austere life of La Trappe. After some years he was sent to Rome, as resident procurator of the order, where I had the pleasure of knowing him. Several amusing anecdotes mingle with his memory, to show how even in his sackcloth and ashes lived his wonted fire.

Among those whom Gregory deservedly called to the highest honours in Rome, was that amiable prodigy Cardinal Joseph Mezzofanti*. When, after the revolution, the city of Bologna sent a deputation to renew its fealty to the Pope, it wisely named as one to compose it, Professor Mezzofanti. The Pope, who had known him before, and was charmed with him, gave him the rank of Prelate, and shortly after brought him to Rome, to reside there permanently. He named him first Warden of the Vatican Library, that is in truth, librarian,—this title being then reserved to a Cardinal—and in February, 1838, raised him to the Cardinalitial dignity.

The name of this eminent man is too well known throughout Europe to require any *eulogium* here. Moreover, a most accurate and full life of him has been compiled by one who has spared no pains or research to make the biography complete. I allude to the Very Reverend Dr Russell, President of St Patrick's College, Maynooth, to whom I have transferred my little stock of anecdotes and information concerning my good and gifted friend. Having made this sacrifice to the desire of another, who I may describe by the very same terms, I will not anticipate here what will be adorned by the graceful pen of this biographer. I will only say, that I can attest Mezzofanti's perfect utterance and expression in the few languages with which I happen to be acquainted; and that I have heard natives of almost every country in Europe and Asia, not to mention California, who have borne witness in my presence to his perfection in accent and phrase, when sepaking their various languages. The general observation used to be, that they would have easily taken him for a native, each of his own country.

This magnificent gift of universal speech was not thrown away in any sense. It was habitually employed in good; in instructing and assisting spiritually many who, without him, might have remained ignorant or helpless. Though it was natural that he should be fond of conversing in his many languages, I should doubt if ever it was done from love of display; for he was humble and shrinking on every occasion. Indeed he knew his powers to be a gift rather than an acquisition.

His appearance certainly did not bear the seal of his high intellectual mark; for his learning on all subjects was accurate, extensive, and solid. The countenance, which was the dial to the busy and complicated works above it, was not ample, or noble in its traits. His brow was a problem for phrenologists: though his eyes were heavily pressed outwards by what they may have considered lingual faculties. One of his order once told him gravely that he had great facility in learning languages. "But then," Mezzofanti archly added in telling me this wise discovery, "he knew that I was acquainted with fifty." Most amiable too he was, simple and childlike, charitable to excess, and ready to help anyone with head or hand.

At the period of the late republic, he remained in Rome when most of his colleagues retired; his constitution, shaken by age and infirmities, was probably further enfeebled by mental sufferings proceeding from the events of the time: he sank and died March the 12th, 1849. In the brief record of his life given in what may be called the Roman "*Court Guide*" though it does not extend to ten lines, there is a word wanting, the omission of which does not occur in any other such summary for thirty years. Wherever a cardinal

GREGORY THE SIXTEENTH

may have died, even if it was in a village in the Terra di Lavoro, he is stated to have been 'laid in state' (*esposto*) and buried in the church of the place; if in Rome, in his own 'title.' Of Mezzofanti alone this is not said. Yet he died during a commonwealth which proclaimed that genius and virtue were to be honoured in all, wherever found. Did this high dignity, though adorned by every virtue, without a drawback, deprive him of a claim to his share of that boasted impartial homage? Such an exception suffices to throw doubts, at least, on the sincerity of those professions.

When Cardinal Weld passed to a better life, his successor was in everybody's mouth, nor could it have been otherwise. There was only one person qualified in every respect for the dignity. This was Monsignor Charles Acton*, the only Englishman who, in our times, has gone through the regular course of preparation which lead most naturally to the purple. For though his was an English family, it was one well known for a long connection with Naples; where the future cardinal was born, March the 6th, 1803.

His education, however, was in great measure English. For though he learnt his rudiments from M. De Masnod, now bishop of Marseilles, he came to England in 1811, on the death of his father, Sir John Francis Edward. It was at Richmond, in Surrey, that he first was admitted to communion by the Rev. M. Beaumont: he used to relate with great delight, how it was on that happy day, by the banks of the Thames, he formed the decided resolution of embracing the ecclesiastical state. He was then at a Protestant school in Isleworth. From this he was sent to Westminster School, which he was obliged soon to quit on religious grounds. He next resided with a Protestant clergyman in Kent, the Rev. Mr Jones, as a private pupil. After this, in 1819, he went to Cambridge, and became, under Dr Neville, an intimate of Magdalene College, where he finished his secular education in 1823. The reader will allow that this was very unusual preparation for the Roman purple.

He now, in 1823, came to Rome, and entered the college, where ecclesiastics, intending to be candidates for public offices, receive a special training. Here Acton distinguished himself by his piety and assiduity, having, besides the common lectures, the assistance of a private tutor, in Professor, afterwards Cardinal, Fornari*. One of his probational essays attracted such attention from the Secretary of State, Dalla Somaglia*, that Pope Leo XII made him one of his chamberlains, and sent him as an attaché to the Nunciature of Paris. Here he had the best possible opportunity of becoming throughly acquainted with diplomacy.

Pius VIII recalled him to Italy, and named him Vicelegate, giving him the choice of any out of the four legations over which Cardinals presided. This was quite a new office, and Monsignor Acton selected Bologna, as affording him the best opportunities for improvement. Here he became acquainted with the whole system of provincial administration, and the application of civil law. He was, however, but a short while there; for at the close of that brief Pontificate, he left the city, before the unexpected revolution broke out. He was in England again in 1829, to marry his only sister Elizabeth to Sir Robert Throckmorton.

By Gregory XVI he was made an assistant judge in the civil court at Rome, and secretary to the most important congregation, or council, for the maintenance of religious discipline. But in January, 1837, to his own astonishment and dismay, he was appointed to the highest dignity in Rome, after the cardinalate, that of Auditor of the Apostolic chamber. Probably it was the first time that so responsible a post, generally conferred on a prelate of great judicial experience and of long standing, had been offered to a foreigner. Acton refused it, but was obliged to yield to a sovereign command. This office is considered as necessarily leading to a place in the Sacred College; so that when Cardinal Weld died in the April following Acton's promotion, it could hardly be matter of conjecture that his turn was not far distant.

GREGORY THE SIXTEENTH

The death of his elder brother, Sir Ferdinand Acton of Aldenham in Salop, brought him to England in 1837, for a short time, in order to settle family affairs, which he did in the most generous manner. He was proclaimed Cardinal January 24th, 1842, having been created nearly three years before. His health, never strong, soon began to decline; a prolonged attack of ague weakened him till he was unable to shake it off, and he sought refuge, first at Palermo, then in Naples, his native city. But it was too late: and he expired there, June the 23rd, 1847.

Many who saw him knew little of his sterling worth. So gentle, so modest, so humble was he, so little in his own esteem, that his solid judgment, extensive acquirements, and even more ornamental accomplishments, were not easily elicited by a mere visitor or casual guest. It used to be said by those who knew him in early youth, that his musical powers and genial wit used to form, combined, an inexhaustible fund of innocent cheerfulness; and certainly his countenance seemed to have retained the impression of a natural humour that could have been easily brought into play. But this was over-ruled by the pressure of more serious occupations, and the adoption of a more spiritual life.

The soundness of his judgment and his legal knowledge were fully recognised by the bar; for it was familiarly said by advocates of the first rank, that if they could only know Monsignor Acton's view of a case, they could make sure of what would be its ultimate decision. In like manner, when he was officially consulted on important ecclesiastical business, and gave his opinion in writing, this was so explicit, clear, and decisive, that Pope Gregory used to say that he had never occasion to read anything of his twice over.

The greatest proof which the Pope could well have given him of his confidence was to select him, as he did, to be his interpreter and only witness, in the important interview with the late Emperor of Russia. Of what took place at it, not a word was ever breathed by the Cardinal beyond this, that, when he had interpreted the Pope's first sentence, the

Emperor turned to him in the most respectful and finished manner, and said, "It will be agreeable to me if your Eminence will act as my interpreter also." Immediately after the conference, to which allusion will have to be made later, Cardinal Acton wrote down, at the Pope's request, a minute account of it; but he never allowed it to be seen.

The King of Naples came to Rome principally to provide a good bishop for his metropolis, and pressed acceptance of the see on Cardinal Acton, who, however, inexorably refused it. When a lamentable accident deprived the then reigning family of France of its first born, I well remember the bereaved mother[1] wrote to him as a friend in whom she could confide, or tell her griefs and hopes, and obtain through him what could alleviate her sorrows.

As to his charities, they were so unbounded, that he wrote from Naples that he actually tasted the distress that he had often sought to lighten in others. He may be said to have departed hence in all the wealth of a willing poverty.

CHAPTER V

CARDINAL ANGELO MAI

AMONG the worthies of this Pontificate is one who deserves a separate chapter, though it shall not be longer than is absolutely necessary for a very slight sketch. This is Cardinal Angelo Mai, the discoverer of more lost works, and the describer of more ancient manuscripts, sacred and profane, than it has fallen to the share of any other, in modern times, to publish. It may be premised that his real biography has yet to be written.

In the province of Bergamo, part of the Lombardy-Venetian kingdom, is a little mountain village named

---

1. Amelia, wife of King Louis Phillipe, was the daughter of the King of Naples, whose rulers the Acton family had served in high office in that kingdom for several generations.

Schilpario. Here, on the 7th of March, 1774, was born the subject of this brief memoir, who by his will enriched his heirs, "the community of the poor" of his native village. A member of the suppressed order of Jesuits was his first preceptor, and the guide to his future fame. This was Luigi Mozzi*, under whose direction, in the episcopal seminary at Bergamo, he made rapid progress in classical and modern letters. Suddenly, with four school-fellows, he left his native country and repaired to Colorno, in the Duchy of Parma, where Ferdinand of Bourbon, with the consent of Pius VI, had permitted the Society to establish themselves. He joined the order in 1799, and continued his studies with such success that, in 1804, he was sent to Naples as Professor of *Belles-Lettres*.

From Naples he went to Rome for a short time, and thence to Orvieto, at the special desire of its bishop, John Baptist Lambruschini. There he remained some years in retirement, and received the priesthood. Under the tuition of Father Manero and Monchaca, Spanish ex-Jesuits, he made great progress, not only in the ancient languages, Hebrew included, but likewise in the art of palæography which was to win him his highest honours. But, as of old under Augustus Cæsar, there went forth an imperial and imperious edict, that every subject of the 'Italian kingdom' should betake himself to his native province. In obedience to it Mai, accompanied by his Mentor Mozzi, proceeded to Milan.[1]

It was a providential journey; and Mai had reason to thank Napoleon for his stern mandate. And so, perhaps, has the 'republic of letters,' whatever hostility that title may imply to all despotic commands. Mozzi, fully acquainted with the powers and acquirements of his pupil, had him named a doctor of the Ambrosian library. The magnificent collection of

---

1. He had quitted the Society, which was scarcely established anywhere, with the full consent and approbation of its superiors; especially of the venerable and saintly F. Pignatelli.

manuscripts, which form its chief treasure, is mainly due to the munificence of Cardinal Frederick Borromeo*, nephew and almost rival of the great St Charles. He sent learned men all over the world to purchase manuscripts, or have them diligently copied. Among other sources of additional literary wealth had been the famous monastery of Bobbio, founded by the Irish St Columbanus in the seventh century, the manuscripts of which had been divided between the Ambrosian and the Vatican libraries.

The period for the study of manuscripts might be said to have passed; at least in the noblest sense of the word. The known manuscripts of some given author, the twenty Homers, or the five Demosthenes, or the two hundred Testaments, which a great library was known to possess, might be looked through twice in a century for a new edition, 'coll.Cod.,' of '*Cum variantibus Lectionibus ex Codd.MSS.*' But the hunt after new, or rather old, works of ancient authors, in the manuscript rooms of libraries, was quite as much given up as falconry in the modern chase. To revive it was reserved for Angelo Mai.

He found in the Milanese library an unexplored mine. No doubt its manuscripts had been catalogued, perhaps described, and that accurately. But those who had preceded him had only cultivated the upper soil in this literary field. They had not discovered the exuberantly precious 'royalties' which lay hidden beneath the surface. Under the letter of the writing there slumbered a spirit which had long lain there spell-bound, awaiting a master-magician to free it: a spirit of poetry sometimes, sometimes of eloquence; a muse of history, a genius of philosophy, a spirit of merest unsubstantial elegance.

To drop figures, the peculiarity of Mai's wonderful discovery consisted in the reading of manuscripts twice written; or, as they are more scientifically called, palimpsests.[1]

A book, for instance, may have been properly catalogued

1. From the vellum having been scraped again, to prepare it for second writing.

GREGORY THE SIXTEENTH

as containing the commentaries or sermons of some abbot of the eleventh or twelfth century, works of which there may be several other transcripts in the library. Edited or not, it is improbable that the volume has been, or will be, looked into during a generation. But the lens-like eye of a Don Angelo peers into it, and it becomes a treasure trove. The writer of the middle ages had taken down from the shelves a work which he considered of small value—perhaps there were duplicates of it—some letters, for instance, of a heathen emperor to his tutor; and had scrubbed, as he thought, the parchment clean both of its inky and of its moral denigration; and then had written over it the recent production of some favourite author.

It is this under-writing that Mai scanned with sagacious eye; and perhaps it was like the lines of a repainted canvass, which in the course of time come through the evanescent tints superadded; a leg or arm cropping out through the mouth of an impassioned head by the second artist; and he could trace clearly the large forms of uncial letters of the fourth or fifth century, sprawling through two lines of neatly written brevier. Or the scourging had been more thoroughly done; and then a wash of gallic acid revived the pallid reed-strokes of the earlier scribe.

Ingenuity, patience, learning, and immense perseverance were requisite for the process. Often only unconnected passages were found; half a sentence on one page, which the next did not continue, but the rest of which might perhaps be found in another manuscript three hundred numbers off; sometimes portions of various works were jumbled together under one later production, upside down, back to back, like shuffled cards; while, perhaps, not one page contained the "*Incipit*," of the "*Explicit feliciter liber I de*———," so as to give a clue to what these fragments contained. Learning was then indeed necessary; for conjecture often gave the first inclination of what had been discovered from the style, or from the sentence having been fortunately embalmed or petrified, by quotation in some later author.

In this way did Mai labour on, looking through the tangled mass of confused materials, catching up the ends of different threads, and pursuing them with patient diligence, till he had drawn each, broken or perfect as it happened to exist.

After one minor publication of a translation, he began in 1813, and continued till 1819, to pour out an unintermitting stream of volumes, containing works or portions of works, lost, as it was supposed irrecoverably. Various orations of Cicero; the lost wrtings of Julius Fronto; unpublished letter of Marcus Aurelius, Antonius Pius, Lucius Verus, and Appian; fragments of speeches by Aurelius Symmachus; the history of Dionysius of Halicarnassus from the 12th to the 20th book; unedited fragments of Philo; ancient commentaries on Virgil; two books of Eusebius' Chronicles; the intineries of Alexander, and of Constantius Augustus, son of the Emperor Constantine; three books of Julius Valerius on the Actions of Alexander the Great; the 6th and 14th Sibylline books; finally, the celebrated Gothic version, by Ulphilas, of St Paul and other parts of Scripture.

Such were the principle works recovered and published, with notes, prefaces, and translations, by this indefatigable scholar, in the period just mentioned of six years. It was work in which he could have little or no assistance from others; in fact it was an art exclusively his own.

Mai's reputation was already European. At the early age of thirty-seven he had made more additions to our stock of ancient literature than a century had done before him. At this moment a vacancy occurred in the Vatican library, that of first librarian. Cardinals Consalvi* and Litta*, the Secretary of State and Head-Librarian, at once cast their eyes on the young priest at Milan, as the fittest person to occupy the post.

On his arrival in Rome he lost no time in exploring the wider and richer field offered to his cultivation. He came no longer to learn; but with a perfected tact, an experienced eye, and a decisive critical judgment. Hence he soon began his work of reproduction, and, singularly enough, in continuation of his previous successes. For he discovered in the Vatican, portions of the very Bobbio manuscripts which he had explored in the Ambrosian; containing consequently the wanting parts of authors already partially recovered.

This was the case with Fronto and his imperial pupils and friends, one of the most charming epistolary collections ever published. By adding what was in Rome to what had been given at Milan, Mai was able to present a much more complete edition of it. He also published valuable fragments of civil law, anterior to the Justinian code, and of works on orthography by comparatively obscure authors.

But what he had till now performed was eclipsed by the most fortunate and brilliant of his discoveries;—that of Cicero's long-coveted treatise "*De Republica*." Petrarca, Poggio, and Bessarion, with a host of elegant scholars, had desired and sought in vain to see this treatise. It had eluded every research. Under a copy of St Augustine's *Commentary on the Psalms* Mai had discovered it, in large bold characters, with its title legible.

I can well remember the commotion which the announcement of this success excited through the literary world in Rome. Of course it took some time to prepare the work for publication. Indeed I have heard from the learned discoverer himself, that, while new types were being cast, and arrangements made for publishing it through all Europe, he was busily engaged in hunting out all the quotations of Cicero's work dispersed through the ponderous tomes of subsequent writers, especially Fathers.

The very one whose own lucubrations had shielded it from destruction, and covered it with a patina or antiquarian crust such as often saves a valuable medal, yielded no small number of extracts, which either were found in the discovered portions and so verified their genuineness, or were absent from them and so filled up *lacunae*.

How often have I had that precious volume in my hand, with the man whose fame it crowned explaining to friends around him the entire process of discovery, and the manner in which he drew out order from the chaotic confusion of its leaves. Indeed seldom has it been my lot to lead any party to visit the Vatican library while Monsignor Mai was librarian, without his leaving his own pursuit, to show us its treasures, and, not the least valuable of them, himself.

It need not be said that further honours and promotions were lavished upon him. He was made Canon of St Peter's, a burthen indeed, but a distinction also; and a prelate of the highest order. Gregory XVI, wishing to employ his extraordinary abilities in the service of religion, named him Secretary of the Congregation of Propaganda. This was in 1833; but, though his office took him away from his dear manuscripts and gave him occupation enough for any other man, it did not interrupt his studies. He was allowed to have the codicies at his house, and went on transcribing and printing as much as before. At length on the 12th of February, 1838, Pope Gregory named him Cardinal, together with his illustrious friend, and successor in the librarianship, Mezzofanti.

Even now, he was appointed to offices that required great attention and assiduity; still there was no intermission in his favourite pursuits. He did not confine his industry to palimpsests; but drew from the shelves of the Vatican, histories, poems, medical and mathematical treatises, acts of councils, biblical commentaries; in fine, works of every age and of every class, classical, patristic, medieval, and even modern; not only in Greek and Latin, but in Arabic, Syro-Chaldaic, and Armenian. He re-established, under the auspicies of Gregory, the celebrated Vatican press, which had formerly published the splendid St Ephrem; he had new types cast for it in various alphabets, from the best models in old manuscripts; and especially employed it in the printing of the great *Codex Vaticanus*, which he transcribed.

GREGORY THE SIXTEENTH

The fruit of this unceasing labour may be summarily described as follows:

1. "*Scriptorum veterum nova collectio.*" A collection, in ten huge quarto volumes, of writers sacred and profane, of every age.

2. "*Classici scriptores ex codicibus Vaticanis editi;*" in ten volumes of smaller dimensions. These two series closely followed one another. The first began to be published in 1827, and the second was closed in 1838.

England was not behind other countries in honouring the genius and indefatigable application of this great man. The Royal Society of Literature awarded him its gold medal in 1824, with this inscription on the reverse: '*Angelo Mai palimpsestorum inventori et restauratori.*'[1] Literary distinctions showered on him from every side, and his bust was erected in halls of learned societies. His labours, however, did not end here. Finding abundant materials yet remaining at hand, worthy of publication, he undertook and completed:

3. "*Spicilegium Romanum,*" another series of ten volumes, which he finished in 1844.

In 1853(ed. 1854), on the death of Cardinal Lambruschini*, he was named Cardinal-Librarian, though it can hardly be said that this appointment changed his habits, or increased his advantages. Still he continued his work, and commenced the publication of a new series of twelve volumes:

4. "*Nova Patrum Bibliotecha.*" Only six volumes had appeared when death brought his labours prematurely to a close.

This took place on the 8th of September, 1854, after a short inflammatory attack, which lasted thirty-five hours, at Albano, whither he had retired for a change of air. He was calm, resigned, and most devout.

The mere catalogue of the authors, some of whose works he for the first time published, would fill several pages, but

1. [For Angelo Mai, the discoverer and restorer of palimpsests.]

it may be worth mentioning, that, besides the many classical authors whom he thus illustrated, there is not a single century of the Christian era, from the second to the seventeenth, from which he has not produced important and previously unknown works.

He assured me that he had transcribed all with his own hand; translated, if Greek; and added notes and prefaces (generally full of learning) entirely by himself. This, however, was at an earlier period; for in the preface to the second volume of his last work, he mentions the Abbate Matranga as his assistant. He had also the aid of learned Orientals for Eastern manuscripts.

His transcript of the celebrated manuscript of the entire Greek Scripture was printed many years before his death. Why it was not published, nobody but himself seemed to know. A couple of years before his decease, he asked me if he thought any publisher would take the whole impression off his hands, and dispose of it on his own account.

Now, however, it may be judged to have been for the best that the publication was delayed: for in a copy of such a manuscript the most rigorous exactness is the first requisite. Not only a word, but a letter, a sign, a jot or tittle that deviates from it, impairs its value as a representative to a referee in doubtful or difficult passages. Interminable disputes might arise on a reading as presented by the original, on the faith of its copy; and if final appeal is made to the manuscript, and it is found to have been unfaithfully transcribed in one place, all trust is at an end. Now, that in copying so huge and inconvenient a book some slight errors should have been committed, especially when it is done by a person distracted by numerous other undertakings, is only in conformity with a trite axiom, about the natural proneness of humanity.

The work has therefore been minutely collated with the original, by a commission of able scholars; and a list of mistakes have been made extending to fourteen pages. With this accurate correction, the work is offered for

GREGORY THE SIXTEENTH

immediate publication.

The will of this no less estimable and learned man was in his own handwriting, and was remarkable for the kindness of its provisions. All his household were secured their full pay for life if they had been ten years in his service, half pay if they had been six. A large sum, besides, was to be divided among them. For the very poor of his native village he provided an endowment of twelve thousand dollars, besides making them his residuary legatees. To its parish church he bequeathed all his ecclesiastical plate and furniture.

His library, which he describes as large and precious, he says he would have gladly left for the general use of the Roman clergy. But he had not the proper means to provide premises in which to preserve it, or a proper endowment to increase, or sufficient officers to guard it.

He therefore desires it to be valued, and sold; yet, so that, should the Papal Government be disposed to purchase it, the price should be only half its valuation. Even, however, should this be the case, he makes it a condition that his collection be kept apart and bear his name; or at least, that each book should keep his arms already placed within it.

His Manuscripts he left absolutely to the Vatican. It need not be added, that the Pope immediately gave orders for the purchase of the library; which has been placed in an apartment by itself, in the great library over which Mai shed such additional lustre. There Pius IX went to visit it in the carnival of 1856.

A little anecdote is connected with this portion of his will. A few days before his death, while apparently in full possession of his ordinary health, he stopped his carriage at the door of a well-known bookseller, whom he much employed in his book transactions, and asked him if there was any news in his line of business.

The tradesman, with surprise, replied that till the winter nothing would be going on, "Then," said the Cardinal, "you will soon have an extensive job to do."

"What?" it was naturally asked.

"My dear B——," replied Mai, with tears in his eyes, and pressing the hand of his attached client, "you will soon have to value my library. Farewell!"

This circumstance, and his having left, for the first time, the key of his private cabinet, in which were his secret papers, with his executor, Cardinal Altieri, naturally led all to suppose that premonitory symptoms, unseen by others, forewarned him of his approaching dissolution.

His marble monument, which was commenced in his lifetime, is a beautiful specimen of what artists know by the name of the *cinquecento* style.

It is composed of a base from which rise two Corinthian pilasters, flanking a deep niche, and supporting an arch. In the niche is a rich sarcophagus, on which reposes the effigy of the Cardinal, offering up his works, towards which he points, to the Incarnate Wisdom, who is represented in relief on the upper portion of the recess. On each of its walls are medallions representing Mai's nomination to the Ambrosian and Vatican libraries. Above them and below are angels holding scrolls, on which are written in Greek, Latin, Hebrew, and old Syriac, the text of Esdras vii.6, "He was a ready scribe in the law." The Holy Spirit, and the four Latin Doctors of the Church in relief, occupy the inside of the arch; above which, outside, rises the architectural cornice, then a semicircular lunette bearing the Cardinal's arms, and towering above all the triumphant cross.

Among Mai's papers was found his sepulchral inscription, in his own hand. It has been engraven on the base of this monument, now erecting in his titular church of St Anastasia. Benzoni*, one of the most distinguished artists of Rome, is the sculptor chosen by Mai himself for the work. The following is the epitaph carved upon it:—

"*Qui doctis vigilans studiis mea tempora trivi,*
　　Bergomatum soboles, Angelus, hic iaceo,
Purpureum mihi syrma dedit rubrumque galerum
　　Roma; sed empyreum das mihi, CHRISTE, polum.
Te expectans, longos potui tolerare labores;
　　Nunc mihi sit tecum dulcis et alta quies!"

The indulgent reader will, perhaps, accept the following for a translation:

I, who my life in wakeful studies wore,
　　Bergamo's son, named Angelo, here lie.
The purple robe and crimson hat I bore
　　Rome gave: Thou giv'st me, CHRIST! the empyreal sky.
Awaiting Thee, long toil I could endure
　　So that with Thee my rest be sweet, secure!"

This epitaph makes known the man, not unconscious, indeed, of his great parts, nor of their noble devotion; not blind to his life-long assiduity and its well-earned success; but still consistent, in all and throughout all, with the principles, the thoughts, and the conduct of a true ecclesiastic. Thus Mai, eminently was, from youth to old age; adorned with every priestly virtue, modest and humble; so that speak to him of his own great works, and he turned you away from the topic with a blush and gentle disclaimer, which was manifestly sincere.

His habits were most simple and temperate. He rose very early, and after Mass sat down to his books before six, and studied the whole morning, with the interruption of a light meal. Of course, at one period of his life, both before and after his cardinalate, he had official audiences to give; and he never was absent from any religious service at which others of his rank attended. Still every moment that could be snatched from these duties, which were always thoroughly discharged, was seized for his favourite pursuits; and

I should doubt if, during the few moments that a secretary might take in going to the next room for a paper, and returning with it, a line was not copied or translated from the open manuscript on the table.

He rarely went into society, except for a few minutes, where courteous duty imperatively demanded it. A solitary drive, which I have sometimes counted it an honour to deprive of that epithet, perhaps a short walk, was almost all the robbery that he permitted recreation to make from his domestic converse at home with that chaste wisdom that had early captivated his heart. Soon after dusk, his servants were dismissed, his outer door was inexorably bolted, and alone with his codices he was lavish of his midnight oil, protracting his studies to an unknown hour.

This retirement and uncongeniality with society obtained for him, with those who did not know him, a character of moroseness or haughtiness, which disappeared the moment you approached him. He was most affable, kind, and ready to assist by counsel or suggestion: and, however interrupted in his own work, he never betrayed impatience or a desire to get rid of the visit. His countenance, perhaps, encouraged with some that misinterpretation of his character. A most noble forehead, equal to containing, piled up but orderly within, any amount of knowledge, caught the eyes of the visitor to a Papal function, and generally inspired the desire to know whose countenance it distinguished. Then came eyes deeply burrowing under brows knitted somewhat by the effort which a short-sighted person makes to see, till he has rendered habitual the expression of that strain.

His features were dignified, modelled on a firm intellectual type. And undoubtedly his conversation was serious; to a beholder severe, but not to a listener. One naturally spoke to him on grave subjects, loved to learn from his conversation, listened with respect—with reverence rather—and felt in the presence of a virtuous and a wise man, with whom it would be a pride one day to have been familiar.

GREGORY THE SIXTEENTH

But there was not a particle of superciliousness, or overbearing, or sarcastic manners about him; none of the oppressiveness of genius, or the ponderousness of rare learning. Yet both the learning and the genius were discernible in everything he wrote. His manner was calm and earnest, but unimpassioned; persuasive and eloquent, without clamour. His published discourses are specimens of beautiful diction and noble thoughts.

One very common imputation cast upon him, however, was a want of liberality in permitting others to share his advantages. It used to be commonly said, that he shut the Vatican to scholars, especially those from foreign countries, who wished to collate manuscripts from some particular work. Speaking from personal experience, I can only say that I never either felt or observed that failing. I found him at all times, not merely obliging, but extremely kind; and was permitted to examine, to collate, and to copy or trace any manuscripts that I required, or wished to study.[1]

And I have generally seen the great reading room of the Library crowded with scholars busy upon codices. Mere idlers, or persons who came with no definite object, it is very probable that he would not encourage; but I should doubt that any great classical work has been published in our time, which is deprived of the advantages derivable from Roman manuscripts, in consequence of such a refusal to examine them; or

1. As early as 1827 these feelings were openly expressed by me in the following passage:—"Neque pariter silentio praetermittendus Vir toto literario orbi clarus, Ill. Angelus Mai, sub cujus auspticiis Bibliothecae Vaticanae κειμηλια Syriaca evolvi; quique, quum nihil a se alienum putet quod litteris sacris profanisque, quas omnes dum colit, exornat, possit bene-vertere, me in his studiis aliquid proficere conantem, jam non dicam humanitate, sed et benevolentia est prosecutus." Horae Syriacae, Praef. p. xiii.

[I must not pass over in silence a man who is well known throughout the world, that most distinguished scholar, Angelo Mai. It was under his auspices that I studied the Syrian treasures of the Vatican Library. There was nothing in sacred and profane literature that was outside his ken. When I was trying to achieve some proficiency in these studies, which he cherishes, embellishes and could turn to advantage, he treated me, I will not say merely with humanity, but even with special kindness.]

that any scholar properly recommended ever experienced a rebuff. Like most person, who, working hard themselves, exact full labour from those subject to them, Mai had his murmerers in the Library itself; but time has fully justified his exaction of vigilance and industry from them.

Perhaps we may not ill characterise him and his pursuits, by an amalgamation and adaption of two eulogies by an old poet:—

> Angele Mai, "studiose, memor, celer, ignoratis
>   Assidue in libris, nec nisi operta legens;
> Exesas tineis opicasque evolvere chartas
>   Major quam promptis cura tibi in studiis.
> Aurea mens, vox suada tibi, tum sermo quietus:
>   Nec cunctator eras, nec properante sono.
> Pulchra senecta, nitens habitus, procul ira dolusque,
>   Et placidæ vitæ congrua meta tibi."[1]

Well might Niebuhr* say of him, that he was "a man divinely granted to our age, to whom no one citizen or stranger,—to use the words of Ennius,—will be able to repay the fruits of his labours."[2]

---

1. Again will the courteous reader accept a poor translation?

> "Mai, studious, unforgetting, quick, intent
>   On books long lost,—to trace their covered lines;
> Parchments, worm-gnawed, thy care,—time-soiled and rent,
>   Beyond what lore on modern pages shines;
> Sterling thy mind; winning thy tongue, and sweet;
>   Rapid nor slow thy speech. Fair looked old age
> In thy sheen robes, free from all craft or heat;
>   Meet for thy placid course, its closing stage."

AUSONIUS, Prof. de Victoria et Staphylio.

2. *In Vita Agathiae.*

CHAPTER VI

CHARACTER OF GREGORY THE SIXTEENTH

THERE is yet living at least one English nobleman, celebrated for his love of art, who saw Pius VII when elected Pope at Venice in 1800. It may be doubted if there be a second person in the United Kingdom whose recollection of Pontiffs reaches as far back. There are hundreds, however, if not thousands, who remember Gregory XVI; who have been presented to him, and who consequently retain distinct impressions of his looks, his address, and his conversation. Scarcely as Englishman, whose travels were performed during his long Pontificate, left Rome without this honour and gratification. Upon such points, therefore, as merely meet the eye, recollections of him may be spread over the whole country, and, indeed, to exist in one generation or other of every travelled family.

The remarks one heard from such outside observers were, that at first sight his features did not seem cast in so noble a mould as those of his predecessors; they were large and rounded, and wanted those finer touches which suggest ideas of higher genius or delicate taste. But this judgment ceased the moment you came into closer contact and conversation with him. He did not discourse freely in any languages but Italian and Latin; and, therefore, persons who had to communicate with him through an interpreter, and to have each sentence repeated twice, such, for example, as the late Baron Kestner,[1] could form a very imperfect opin-

1. Prussian Ambassador in Rome.

ion of his conversational powers.

But those who could speak Italian freely, and approached him merely to receive his blessing, soon found him launch into familiar conversation, which drew them almost into forgetfulness of his twofold dignity. His countenance then, and still more when discoursing on graver topics, lighted up, and was mantled with a glowing expression; his eyes became bright and animated, and his intelligence and learning gave themselves utterance through his flowing and graceful language. I remember an Englishman of letters who got upon the subject of poetry in his audience, and came away struck by the Pope's judicious observations, as well as extensive and familiar acquaintance with his theme.

In health he was robust, and his powers of exertion, physical and mental, were great. He could tire out most of his attendants in his daily walks. His favourite one was beyond Pontemolle along the old Flaminian way to Torre di Quinta, a considerable distance; and he enjoyed seeing much younger men glad to remount their horses or their carriages to return home.

His health was, indeed, so hale and sound, on his accession, that he declined naming any physician or surgeon for his own person, but ordered the salaries of those offices, and others which he similarly kept in abeyance, to be invested, towards forming a superannuation fund for the servants and officers of the palace. This he nursed and increased till it became of considerable amount.

After a few years, however, a cancerous affection attacked his face; and in 1835, by advice of the Prussian minister, he sent for an able physician, Dr Alertz of Aix-la-Chapelle, with whom I happened to travel on board a steamer, in company with Dr Reumont, for many years attached to the Prussian embassy at Florence, and well known in art-literature, for his able writings on Andrea del Sarto. The young German, acting with the Italian physician to the palace, arrested the progress of the disease, so that it does not seem to have acted on Gregory's constitution or shortened the fulness of his days.

This strength of frame and soundness of organs enabled the Pope, throughout his reign, to attend to business, temporal and ecclesiastical, with unwearying assiduity and unvarying cheerfulness. The severer habits of his claustral life had inured him to the regularity and even monotony of the Papal, its early hours, its seclusion from social enjoyment, its silent meals, its many solitary hours, and their unrelated occupation.

He commenced his morning so truly matutinally that he dispensed with the attendance of a chaplain at his own Mass, saying that it was unreasonable to expect other persons to accommodate themselves to his unseasonable hours. His own servant alone assisted him.

A peculiar simplicity of habits was remarkable in him. When he was Cardinal-Prefect of Propaganda I often noticed this; and how he would do himself what ordinarily a servant might have been called to perform. Hence, while he provided richly for the splendour of divine worship, and replaced some of its plundered ornaments, he would wear nothing costly himself.[1]

His vigorous mind, as has been observed, seemed to shrink from no amount of application to business of every class. It was no idle life, indeed, that he led. In the manner of ecclesiastical affairs business is divided among congregations, or boards as we should call them; but the ultimate result, in every important case, depends on the Papal approbation. It was not uncommon for Gregory to hesitate in giving his assent, to have the papers in the cause brought to himself, and finally to come to a different conclusion from that of the congregation.

Cardinal Acton used to say that he had known as many as eight or ten cases in which the Pope refused to ratify the judgment of a congregation, and had at length reversed it,

---

1. Such as shoes richly embroidered, in accordance with the practice of the Pope's wearing the cross upon it.

upon canonical grounds which had been overlooked by the many learned persons previously engaged in its discussion. And this instinctive perception occurred in cases affecting different countries.

One instance related to Canada. A distinguished bishop of that country found that the Pope demurred to a resolution passed by Propaganda about it; and in a few days, as he declared, fresh information arrived which fully justified the correctness of the sovereign judgment.

A similar instance referred to Germany. I remember that on one occasion being admitted on a day of privacy, I found he was writing a long Latin letter to a bishop in Germany, which he most condescendingly read to me; and masterly it was in sentiment and expression. It produced, indeed, its intended effect, though it involved one of the rarest exercises of Pontifical authority. In like manner he wrote, himself, an answer of several sheets, and sent his own autograph copy, to one of the bishops in England, on a matter which related to an ecclesiastical affair of this country.

In the beginning of his reign long edicts were published on the turbulence and disorder of the times, full of touching appeals and generous sentiments, which, I believe, were considered as the productions of his own pen. In cases of life and death, the silence of the Pope, on the report of the trial being submitted to him by the chief judge, is equivalent to a ratification of the sentence, which then takes its course.

But Gregory always desired the entire pleadings and depositions to be brought to him, and went carefully through them himself: and if he made no observation in returning the papers, it was understood that he tacitly approved the fatal sentence. Oftener, however, he leaned to the side of mercy; and executions were rare and only for atrocious crimes. I am not aware that there was a single execution for political causes in his Pontificate.

In the discharge of his high duties he respected not the

person of man, and cared nothing for the pride and strength of those whom he had to encounter. To one great contest which he sustained, allusion has been made under the last Pontificate,[1] and it is not intended to take up the thread of its narrative in this. It may be sufficient to say that in its last phase, the imprisonment of the Archbishop of Cologne, he fully sustained his character for unflinching support of the cause commited to the protection of his sublime office. Indeed scarcely a year of his Pontificate passed by, without his having to pronounce an allocation on the oppression of the Church in some country or other, north or south of Europe, east or west of the world. He spoke the truth plainly and publicly; and generally reaped the fruit of his straightforwardness and courage.

The most painful of his conflicts, however, was one, face to face, with the greatest of Europe's sovereigns, a man accustomed to command without contradiction, and to be surrounded by complete submission. He did not imagine that there was a human being who would presume to read him a lesson, or still less to administer a rebuke to him.

It may be proper to premise that the present Emperor of Russia, while Czarowich, visited Rome, and was received with the utmost respect by all ranks, and with extreme kindness by the Pope. The young prince expressed himself highly gratified by his reception; and I was told by those to whom he had declared it, that he had procured a portrait of Gregory, which he said he should always keep, as that of a friend deeply venerated and esteemed.

Further, in 1842, the Emperor, his father, had sent a very splendid present to the Pope, a vase of malachite, now in the Vatican library, and a large supply of the same precious material for the Basilica of St Paul. Still he had not ceased to deal harshly, not to say cruelly, with his Catholic subjects, especial-

1. Wiseman alludes to the issue of mixed marriages in Germany on which Pius VIII was consulted by the German bishops. See *Leo XII and Pius VIII*, Fisher Press, 2005, pp. 121-4.

ly the Poles. They were driven into the Greek communion, by putting it out of their power to follow their own worship; they were deprived of their own bishops and priests, and even persecuted by most violent inflictions and personal suffering.

On this subject the Holy See had both publicly and privately complained; but no redress, and but little, if any alleviation, had been obtained. At length, in December, 1845, the Emperor Nicholas I came himself to Rome. It was observed, both in Italy and, I believe, in England, how minute and unrelaxed were the precautions taken to secure him against any danger of conspiracy: how his apartment, bed, food, body-guard, were arranged with a watchful eye to the prevention of any surprise from hidden enemies.

Be this as it may, nothing amiss befell him, unless it was his momentous interview with the Head of that Church which he had mercilessly persecuted, with him whose rival he considered, himself, as the real autocratic Head of a large proportion of what he called the 'Orthodox Church,' and as recognised protector of its entire communion.

It was arranged that the Emperor should be attended by M. de Bouteneff, his minister at Rome, and that the Pope should have a Cardinal at his side. He selected, as has been said, the English Cardinal Acton. This was not a usual provision for a royal visit, but it gave it rather the air of a conference; and so in truth it was. The Pope felt he had a solemn and trying duty to perform. Could he allow the persecutor of his flock to approach him, and depart without a word of expostulation and vein of reproof? Could he receive him with a bland smile and insincere accolade; and speak to him of unmeaning topics of the hour, or of the cold politics of the world?

Impossible! It would have been at variance, not merely with his personal disposition, but with the spiritual character which he held of Father of the Faithful; Defender of the weak; Shepherd of the ravened flock; Protector of the persecuted; Representative of fearless, uncompromising,

GREGORY THE SIXTEENTH 63

martyred Pontiffs; Vicar of Him who feared not the stalking, any more than the prowling, wolf.

It would have been to his conscience a gnawing and undying reproach, if he had lost the opportunity of saying face to face what he had written and spoken of one absent, or if he had employed his privilege as a sovereign to second his mission as a Pontiff. He would have confirmed by his cowardice or his forbearance, though it might be called courtly refinement or gentleness of character, all the self-confidence and fearlessness of a fanatical persecutor, placed above all but some great moral control.

Certainly much hung in the balance of that Pontiff's deliberation, how he should act. The meekest of men, Pius VII had not neglected the opportunity of his captivity, to enumerate, with fervid gentleness, to his powerful oppressor the evils which the Church had suffered at his hands. Gregory never undertook any grave work without much prayer; and one so momentous as this was assuredly not determined on, except after long and earnest supplication.

What were the Emperor's intentions, what his ideas, what his desires in coming to Rome and having necessarily a personal meeting with the Pope, it is impossible to conjecture. Did he hope to overcome him by his splendid presence, truly majestic, soldier-like, and imperial? Or to cajole and win him by soothing speeches and insincere promises? Or to gain the interpretative approval of silence or forbearance?

One must conjecture in vain. Certain it is, that he came, he saw, and conquered not. It has already been mentioned, that the subject and particulars of the conference were never revealed by its only witness at Rome. The Pope's own account was brief, simple, and full of conscious power. "I said to him all that the Holy Ghost dictated to me."

And that was not spoken vainly, with words that had beaten the air, but that their strokes had been well placed and driven home, there was evidence otherwise recorded. An English gentleman was in some part of the palace through which the Imperial visitor passed, as he returned from his interview, and described his altered appearance. He had entered with his usual firm and royal aspect, grand as it was, with statue-like features, stately frame, and martial bearing; free and at his ease, with gracious looks and condescending gestures of salutation. So he passed through the long suite of ante-rooms, the Imperial eagle, glossy, fiery, "with plumes unruffled, and with eye unquenched," in all the glory of pinions which no flight had ever wearied, of beak and talon which no prey had yet resisted.

He came forth again, with head uncovered, and hair, if it can be said of man, dishevelled; haggard and pale; looking as though in an hour he had passed through the condensation of a protracted fever; taking long strides, with stooping shoulders, unobservant, unsaluting: he waited not for his carriage to come to the foot of the stairs, but rushed out into the outer court, and hurried away from apparently the scene of a discomfiture. It was the eagle dragged from his eyrie among the clefts of the rocks, "from his nest among the stars,"[1] his feathers crumpled, and his eye quelled, by a power till then despised.

But let us be fully just. The interview did not excite rancorous or revengeful feelings. No doubt the Pontiff's were in the spirit of those on the High Priest's breast-plate—"doctrine and truth;" sound in principle and true in fact. They convinced and persuaded. Facts with their proofs had, no doubt, been carefully prepared, and could not be gainsayed.

The strong emotion which Gregory on other occasions easily betrayed, could not have been restrained on this. Often in prayer has every beholder seen the tears running down his glowing countenance; often those who have approached him with a tale of distress, or stood by when news of a crime has been communicated to him, have seen his features quiver, and his eye dim with the double sorrow of the Apostle, the tear of weakness with the weak, the scalding drop of indignation for sin.[2] This sensibility cannot have

1. Abdias (Obadiah), 4.
2. 2 Corinthians xi, 29.

been stemmed, even by the coldness of an interpreted discourse, but must have accompanied that flow of eloquent words to which, when earnest, Gregory gave utterance.

All this must have told effectually, where there could be nothing to reply. Mistaken zeal, early prejudice, and an extravagance of natural feelings, had no doubt influenced the Czar towards his Catholic subjects, against the better impulses of his own nature, which Russians always considered just, generous, and even parental. No one had before possessed the opportunity, or the courage, to appeal to the inward tribunal of this better sense. When well made such a call could hardly fail.

> "*Prima est hæc ultio, quod, se*
> *Judice, nemo nocens absolvitur, improba quamvis*
> *Gratia fallaci prætoris vicerit urna.*"[1]

From that interview the Catholics of Russia may date a milder treatment, and perhaps a juster rule.

Other instances may be given of Gregory's firmness in dealing with cases requiring that virtue as well as prudence. Such was the cutting up, root though not branch, of a man already mentioned as giving promise at one time of being leader, as he had been founder, of a magnificent politicoreligious school in France, the Abbé de Lamennais*. By the Encyclical of June 25, 1834 (*Singulari nos*), he condemned the *Paroles d'un Croyant*, and thereby tore off the mask from him who soon exhibited himself to wondering and weeping thousands in his true aspect.

Similarly did he deal with a different school, that of Hermes*, in Germany, the errors of which were purely theological, and of a rationalistic tendency. It was seriously affecting ecclesiastical education on the Rhine; for it was supported by professors of unimpeachable conduct, and usu-

1. Juvenal, Satire XVIII, 1-2. [In the first place, this is the punishment of the guilty man: he cannot escape the verdict of his own heart even though he may have suborned the judge with bribery to give judgment in his favour.]

ally sound doctrine. The creeping error was crushed in its infancy, after much discussion and much forbearance.

Kindness and considerateness were indeed discernible in all the Pope's actions. His charities were in full conformity with the traditions and instincts of his See.

Scarcely, if ever, is a year of his Pontificate unmarked by some private contribution on a large scale to one object of compassion or another. He elevated much the scale, and enlarged the basis, of the magnificent establishment, industrial and eleemosynary, of San Michele a Ripa, in which are collected under one roof every class of sufferers, male and female, from decrepit and helpless old age down to children, from the inmates of the reformatory to those of the nursery; and every sort of industry, from the painter, sculptor, and engraver, to the weaver, the shoemaker, and the carpenter. Under the liberal management of Cardinal Tosti, and the special patronage of Gregory, who annually visited the establishment to inspect its productions in art and in manufactures, and gave it large orders, this has become one of the happiest combinations of charity's well-organised functions.

And the same is to be said of another equally important receptacle for poor children of a lower order, at the Termini, that is, *Thermæ* of Diocletian. This had fallen much into decay; but partly through the munificence, more still under the fostering care of the Pope, it received a new development, which it only wanted the perfecting hand of his successor to carry to its highest attainable completeness.

The prolonged reign of this Pontiff, from 1831 to 1846, presented sufficient opportunities for exercising that charity which the right hand cannot conceal from the left. Thus from October the 26th, 1831, to the beginning of 1834, successive shocks of earthquakes destroyed many houses and villages in Umbria, and shook almost to pieces cities with their sumptuous buildings.

I remember travelling through the province not long after, and witnessing the frightful effects. Some villages through which the road passed—and many more among the hills—were utterly destroyed; though providentially the loss of life was not in proportion to material demolition. Foligno was so shattered, that, excepting the solid cathedral and a few other public buildings, there was not an edifice which was not shored up; and in fact the main street was traversed, through its whole length, by beams, which made the out-thrust and bulging walls on either side give mutual support. And now the traveller will see wall-plates all along, to which interior iron tie-rods are attached; binding every house within.

But the most signal and afflictive overthrow was that of the noble sanctuary of Santa Maria degli Angeli, the dome of which, towering in the plain or valley of Perugia, just below Assisi, was a beautiful object. This dome covered the celebrated Porziuncola, or Chapel of St Francis, the small rural oratory in which he began the work of his stupendous Institute. The entire nave fell in, leaving the cupola marvellously suspended over the little sanctuary, not a brick of which was displaced.[1]

Subscriptions for the many sufferers by this calamity were immediately opened, with the Pope at the head. As to the church, although he and many others contributed largely, the great merit of patient and persevering almsgiving belongs to a simple Francisan lay-brother of the house which served the church, Br. Luigi Ferri, of Bologna; who went from country to country begging contributions, in place of which he often received, and patiently endured, rebuffs and insults, and occasionally the impostor's meed in

1. On being cleaned, one end of this chapel was found to have been painted in fresco by Pietro Perugino, and cut down, so as to mutilate the picture. Overbeck has executed a most lovely painting on the other end, representing a heavenly vision showering flowers on St Francis in prayer. It is well known by its engraving. He lived some years like one of its members in the convent attached, while he finished his work, refusing all other remuneration. See *Dublin Review*, vol.1 p. 458. He had begun his work in 1830.

prison and police-courts. He collected sixteen thousand dollars. The church was completely restored and solemnly reopened in forty months.

Again, when the cholera epidemic appeared in Ancona, a city which had shown itself particularly hostile to him. Gregory sent, from his own resources, considerable relief.

His more private charities are known to have been profuse: but there was one form, though a more spiritual one, which was peculiarly exhibited. On one occasion a Spanish lady, perplexed in conscience, desired to unburthen its anxieties to him as chief pastor; and Gregory descended into the confessional for her, to discharge the functions of a simple priest.

And a German lady of great information and ability, the Baronness K——, informed me, how, being still a Lutheran, but drawn singularly towards the Catholic Church, she asked for an opportunity of placing her difficulties for solution before the Sovereign Pontiff, as its highest authority; and it was instantly granted. He received her in his garden; and, ordering his attendants to remain in one place, walked up and down with her in their presence till he had solved her doubts, and given her his blessing. She was afterwards one of the most zealous co-operators with the Princess Borghese, in supporting the cholera orphans.

And now to come nearer home, he ever showed more than kindness towards those who represented our country in Rome. Having been Prefect of Propaganda for so many years he had become minutely acquainted with every part of the British dominions, both at home and abroad; with its bishops, its wants, its actual condition and future prospects.

A singular instance of his sagacity in this knowledge may be quoted. Not only did he increase, as has been said, the number of Apostolic Vicariates in England, but spontaneously, without being led to it, he told the writer that the hierarchy would have been established here, upon the removal of one obstacle, which he especially described, and emphatically characterised, and which it was not in his power to deal with. When that should occur, he distinctly remarked, this form of church government must be introduced in England.

In the course of a few years, but after his death, the event to which he pointed took place, with consequent circumstances which ordinarily he could not have foreseen; and his successor, unapprised of that forethought, almost at once executed what Gregory had intended under similar conditions.

The Irish College had special motives of gratitude to this Pontiff. The late venerable Bishop of Dromore, then the Rev Dr Michael Blake, parish priest in Dublin, came to restore this establishment, which had been first suppressed under the French occupation, and then incorporated with the College of Propaganda.

The old building on the Quirinal Hill was considered unsuitable, or probably was unavailable for the purpose; and Pope Leo XII by his Brief *"Plura inter collegia,"* of February the 14th, 1826, assigned for the new college a small house, formerly the Umbrian College, situated in the street, Delle botteghe oscure, with a very small church annexed. Dr Blake governed the College till he resigned it into the hands of the Rev Dr Boylan, who in his turn was succeeded by the present Archbishop Cullen*.

Dr Blake was created Bishop of Dromore in 1833; and I rejoice to see him yet vigorously discharging the duties of his office. The following history of his own early career, given by one intimately connected with this admirable house, can hardly fail to edify my readers. When a student at Rome, he was remarkably slow and considered dull. This was owing, perhaps entirely, to considerable indistinctness in his speech, accompanied by hesitation. On one occasion, venturing to interpose his opinion in some discussion among his comrades, one of them rudely interrupted him by saying: "What business have you to speak, who are the dunce of the college?"

The wound was smarting but salutary. The meek boy did not reply, but retired heart-sore into solitude. He reflected on what had been said publicly to him, without rebuke from any one, with silent concurrence of all. Yes, that was his character among them, that the opinion even of the kindest of his friends. If they had not told him of it, one had let it out to him. To this rough monitor he ought to be thankful, for telling him the truth. And now what was to be done? The reproach must be wiped away, the character reversed. Its causes, real or imaginary, must be cured at any cost. This must be the unremitting task of his school-life; he must never forget it.

He took immediate steps for this purpose. He accordingly wrote on a slip of paper 'The Dunce of the College,' in plain, unmistakable letters, and placed it on his desk, where, unseen by others, it should ever be before his eyes. During the regular hours of application there it was; at times of extra study, while others were at recreation, this stinging goad was at his side. He adopted a slow, deliberate utterance, which accompanied him through life, but which perfectly remedied his original defect.

He soon rose honourably both in his class, and in the estimation of his school-fellows—those severest but most accurate of judges—who, however, knew not of the spell which formed the secret of his success. And so he passed through all the honoured degrees of his sacred profession, to its highest attainable dignity. Often have I found this anecdote useful to encourage a down-hearted student: though, of course, I have concealed the name.

In the year 1836 Gregory XVI bestowed on the Irish College a much more spacious house, with a considerable garden. But what forms its chief prize is the church attached to it, being the old basilica of St Agatha in Suburra, which St Gregory the Great himself tells us, in his *Dialogues*, he cleansed from the taint of Arianism, amidst peculiar and portentous occurrences. It is the diaconal church of Cardinal Antonelli*, who has been liberal in repairing it.

As to the English College, Gregory XVI never failed to

GREGORY THE SIXTEENTH

show it the greatest kindness. Twice he visited it; once while I presided over it, under the following circumstances. By acts of perfectly unsolicited goodness, he had twice placed me in his household as one of his chamberlains, first honorary, and then in full degree. In neither case was the act of grace heard of till accomplished, nor in either was any fee permitted to be paid. This office, to which no emoluments are attached, gave a place in all public functions, the most favourable perhaps for witnessing them.

On the 2nd of February, the anniversary of the Pope's election, I was proceeding to take my place in the Sixtine Chapel, when a voice whispered in my ear, that next day, early, His Holiness intended visiting our house. It was one of his more immediate attendants, who not wishing us to be taken by surprise, gave timely warning; otherwise we should have received notice in the evening, without time to make suitable preparations.

Accordingly everything was got ready in time. The College, which is a noble edifice, has a suite of large halls, well fitted for even a Papal reception. The first had just been adorned with what was till then unseen in Rome, a collection of large maps hung on rollers, brought from England; the second contained a number of valuable paintings; the third was the library. In the first a throne was erected, on which the Pope received the inmates of the house, and a few friends brought hastily together.

One good thing on such occasions is that there is no address to be presented, and no formal answer to be given; no tax, in other words, on the resources of commonplace, and no study to say as much as possible on the one side and as little as possible on the other. An easy familiarity and freedom marks all such intercourse between sovereign and subjects. The innocent repartee, the pleasant anecdote, still more the cheery laugh, are not prohibited or witheld.

The function of the throne, therefore, was soon over, and Gregory, seated in the library, was in a short time talking in his usual good-natured strain with all around him. Somehow or other he had received notice of many other importations from England, which had been made by me in a visit to this country in 1836, and he expressed his intention of seeing them all.

So he visited every part of the house, enjoying with evident glee many things of outlandish use, none more than the beer-machine adapted for the purpose of uplifting the produce of the vine, instead of that of the bine. And scarcely less object of amusement was a gigantic medicine-chest, which the master-craftsman in such wares, in London, declared to have been the largest and completest he had ever manufactured, the next having been one for the Emperor of Morocco. The bottles containing the inscrutable compounds of the London pharmacopœia, with their inviting golden labels, the bright finish of every part, the neatness of fit, and the accuracy of packing, almost overcame that involuntary shudder and creeping of the flesh, with which an ordinary mind contemplates a large collection of what in that state, and by those in health, is invariably called physic. It becomes medicine in a small phial by the bed-side.

So passed pleasantly the morning hours, in a loitering cheerful visit, without etiquette or formalities, till the door was reached, and a kind farewell was given, and the royal carriages dashed away towards some other place selected for another of these carnival visits. Of course, the event of the day was not allowed to fade from memory; but was, as usual commemorated and perpetuated by an inscription, as follows:

GREGORI . XVI. PONT. MAX.

CATHOLICAE . RELIGIONIS . PROPAGATORI
QUOD . III. NONAS . FEBRVARIAS . AN. M.D.CCC.XXXVII.
COLLEGIVM . ANGLORUM . INVISENS
ALVMNOSQVE . ADLOQVIO . ET . OMNI . BENIGNITATE . SOLATUS

GREGORY THE SIXTEENTH

STVDIOSISSIMAM . ANIMI . VOLVNTATEM
IN . CATHOLICOS ANGLOS . VNIVERSOS
PVBLICO . HOC . TESTIMONIO . DECLARAVIT.
NICOLAVS . WISEMAN . COLLEGII . RECTOR
IIDEMQVE . ALVMNI
AD . MEMORIAM . AVSPICATISSIMI . DIEI
IN . ANGLORVM . CATHOLICORVM . ANIMIS . ALTE . DEFIXAM
POSTERITATI . COMMENDANDAM
THOMA . WELD . PRESB. . CARD. . PATRONO . SUFFRAGANTE
DEVOTI . SANCTITATI . MAJESTATIQVE . EJVS[1]

Another marble slab records a second visit to the College in 1843; but that is beyond the boundaries of personal recollection.

And now we come to our closing pages, the more difficult in proportion as they are the more agreeable to the writer. For they must be filled up with more personal impressions of this Pontiff's character, distinct from merely official reminiscences. It must be by general observations only that this can be done. Let me then repeat that my acquaintance with this Pope commenced, as it had done with no other before him, while he occupied a subordinate position, and nobody thought of him as a future sovereign.

As Prefect of Propaganda, I had frequently to see him on business, and found him most simple in his habits and kind in his intercourse. The clearness of his views, and quickness of his perception, made it both easy and agreeable to transact business with him. His confidence, once gained upon

1. [For Pope Gregory XVI, a missionary of the Catholic Religion, who on a visit to the English College on the 3rd of February 1837 gave comfort to the students both by his address and by every sign of his goodwill, and indicated in this public testimony the most fervent goodwill in his soul for English Catholics everywhere. Nicholas Wiseman, the Rector and the students of the College have set this up as a memorial of that most happy day in the hearts of English Catholics, and as record of it for posterity. It was placed here with the support of Thomas Weld, Cardinal Priest and Patron of the College in honour of one who is marked with holiness and a royal spirit.]

such subjects as belonged more particularly to one's own sphere, was easily extended to other matters. I could give several instances of this facility; and it was extended to the time of his Pontificate. Not only was an audience easily obtained on ordinary days, and at usual hours, but it was graciously granted almost at any time, when the antechamber was closed, and on days otherwise reserved for private occupation. Indeed it was not uncommon to receive a summons on such days, with an order to proceed to the palace in ordinary dress.

Once I well remember how this familiar kindness served me in great stead. I was engaged in delivering a course of lectures already alluded to, in the apartments of Cardinal Weld, in 1835. They were attended by very large and highly cultivated audiences. On one of the days of delivery I had been prevented from writing the lecture in time, and was labouring to make up for the delay, but in vain. Quarter after quarter of each hour flew rapidly on, and my advance bore no proportion to the matter before me. The fatal hour of twelve was fast approaching, and I knew not what excuse I could make, and how to supply, except by a lame recital, the important portion yet unwritten of my task,—for an index to the Lectures had been printed and circulated.

Just as the last moment arrived, a carriage from the palace drove to the door, with a message directing that I should step into it at once, as His Holiness wished to speak to me. This was indeed a "Deus ex machinâ;" almost the only—and least thought of—expedient that could have saved me from my embarassment. A messenger was depatched to inform the gathering audience of the unexpected cause of a necessary adjournment of our sitting till the next day. The object of my summons was one of very trifling importance; and Gregory little knew what a service he had unintentionally rendered me. "Sic me servavit Apollo."[1]

---

1. [In this way Apollo has served me.]

GREGORY THE SIXTEENTH

But here I must pause. The reception on all such occasions was cordial and most paternal. An embrace would supply the place of ceremonious forms of entrance; at one time a long familar conversation, seated side by side; at another a visit to the penetralia of the Pontifical apartment—a small suite of entresols communicating by an internal staircase—occupied the time.

Here Gregory had his most choice collection of books, from every part of the world, beautifully bound, and many exquisite gems of art, miniatures and copies, as well as original paintings; and here he would ask many questions about English works. What it has been my happiness to hear from him in such visits it would be betraying a sacred trust to reveal. But many and many words then spoken rise to the mind in times of trouble, like stars, not only bright in themselves, but all the brighter in their reflection from the darkness of the mirror.

They have been words of mastery and spell over after-events, promises and prognostics which have not failed, assurances and supports that have never come to nought. Innumerable favours and gracious acts, so many unexpected and unmerited manifestations of goodness, so continued a freedom, or rather familiarity, of communications as I have enjoyed from the condescending kindness of this Pontiff, leave his memory impressed on mine as that of a father rather than a sovereign.

Encouragement, most unrestrained and warm-hearted, in my pursuits, literary or ecclesiastical, however valueless in themselves; proofs of reliance on my fidelity at least, in affairs of greater moment than my own could ever be;—such other marks of favourable sentiments as have been described, painful to me as was the separation from him to which they necessarily led.

All these conspire to make me remember Gregory with a feeling distinct from that which is associated in my mind with any of his predecessors; not with deeper veneration than I entertain for Pius VII; not with warmer gratitude than for

Leo XII; nor with sincerer respect than for Pius VIII; but with a feeling more akin to affection, such as does not often pass the narrow circle that bounds domestic relations. Another sentiment of devotedness and attachment still remains reserved for one whose *eulogium* cannot now, and sincerely do I pray may never, enter for me within the compass of a mere recollection of the past.

Even the close of Gregory's Pontificate, his last years and edifying end, belong not to these imperfect records. If the courteous companions of my journey through the past wish to learn about them, they must consult the common mother of all the Faithful, who treasures up in her better memory the acts and virtues of her Pontiffs and their Fathers.

> "*Hactenus annorum, Comites, elementa meorum*
> *Et memini, et meminisse juvat; —scit cætera Mater.*[1]

STATIUS

---

1. Last lines of Statius' epic poem 'Achilleis.'
[It is up to this point, my friends, that I remember, and take pleasure in recalling the events of my times; my Mother knows the rest.]

ANNEX A

BIOGRAPHICAL SKETCHES

Acton, Cardinal Charles Januarius (1803-47) was born in Naples, the second son of Sir John Acton Bart., who was engaged in Neopolitan trade The family were a cadet branch of the Actons of Aldenham Hall. As Wiseman recounts he was educated privately, then at Westminster School and at Magdalene College, Cambridge. Afterwards he attended the Accademia Ecclesiastica in Rome. An essay he wrote there attracted the attention of Cardinal della Somaglia who was Secretary of State. Leo XII made him a Papal Chamberlain and he was sent as an Attaché to the Nunciature in Paris. Wiseman recounts his subsequent posts in Rome. He was proclaimed Cardinal Priest of Santa Maria della Pace in 1842 and died in Rome.

Agricola, Professor Filippo (1795-1887). His father was a painter and a friend of the sculptor Canova. He himself painted in the style of Raphael, and from 1840 until his death aged 92 he was *Ispettori delle pitture publiche* in Rome.

Albani, Cardinal Giuseppe (1750-1830) was born in Rome. From 1796 till 1814, during the difficulties faced by Pius VI and Pius VII from French interference and occupation of the Papal States, he was in exile in Vienna. He was devoted to the Austrian ruling house, and conveyed its objection to electing Cardinal Severoli as pope. During his exile, in 1801, he was made a Cardinal. On Pius VII's restoration he was given administrative responsibilities in the Vatican.

Altieri, Prince then Cardinal Ludovico (1805-67). The family was of the minor nobility in Rome. Gregory XVI put him in charge of the Civic Guard after the insurrection at the beginning of his reign. He was ordained bishop in 1836. He was Secretary of the Roman Curia and made Cardinal in 1845. After the failed revolution of 1849 he was one of the triumvirate of Cardinals who ruled Rome. He became Prefect of the Roman Curia in 1861.

Antonelli, Cardinal Giacomo (1806-1876). Born of a leading family at Sonnino in the Papal States, he took a law degree at the Sapienza. His first post was as a diplomatic representative of Gregory XVI; later, in 1841, Gregory made him Minister of the Interior. In 1845 he became Treasurer of the Apostolic Camera, and in 1847 he was appointed a Cardinal by Pius IX. In 1848 he was made Secretary of State and remained in this post until his death. He was never a priest.

Baronius, Cardinal Cesare (1538-1607). Ecclesiastical historian. Born at sea, and educated at Veroli and Naples. He joined the Congregation of the Oratory at Rome in 1557 under St Philip Neri whom he succeeded as Superior in 1593. He was made a Cardinal and Vatican Librarian in 1596 by Clement VIII, whose confessor he was. He was twice nearly elected pope, but opposed by Spain because of a book that he had written on the monarchy of Sicily. His best known work, the *Annales Ecclesiastici*, was undertaken at the behest of St Philip Neri to counter an anti-Catholic work, *The Magdeburg Centuries*. The *Annales* treats history in a strictly chronological order, and keeps theology in the background. He coined the phrase "The Dark Ages" to describe the period of early medieval history after the collapse of the Roman Empire in Western Europe.

Belzoni, Giovanni Battista (1778-1823), Egyptologist, traveller and adventurer, was born in Padua. He was ordained a priest but abandoned the clerical state when the French Napoleonic troops invaded Rome. He went to England in 1803, and, when finding himself financially embarassed, earned a living by displaying feats of strength at Astley's Amphitheatre, in which he was served by his huge stature and muscularity. After further travels in Holland, Portugal, Spain and Malta he went to Egypt in 1815. Here he initially worked in hydraulics for Pasha Mohammed Ali. When this proved unsuccessful, he turned to archaeology, discovering the magnificent tomb of Sethos I in the Valley of the Kings in 1817. He acquired busts of Jupiter Memnon which he sent to the British Museum. He made further excavations at the Oasis in Siwa. His work, *Narrative of the Operations and Recent Discoveries in Egypt and Nubia*, was published in English to great acclaim in London in 1821. In the same year he also exhibited a model of the Sethos tomb. While making preparations for an expedition in Africa to travel from Benin to Timbuctoo he died of dysentery in 1823.

Benzoni, Giovan Maria (1799-1873). Sculptor. Born at Clusio (Bergamo). He was a student at the Academy of St Luke where he was influenced by the work of Canova. His own work was often monumental. He was chosen by Cardinal Mai to design and execute his memorial in the Church of Santa Anastasia.

Borghese, Princess Gwendoline (1817-40) was born in Cheltenham, the daughter of John and Maria Teresa Talbot, the 16th Earl and Countess of Shrewsbury. In 1835 she married Prince Marcantonio Borghese. As Wiseman relates, she was active during her short married life in philanthropic work in Rome.

Borromeo, Cardinal Frederico (1563-1631). He was the son of Count Giulio Borromeo and a nephew of St Carlo Borromeo. He was ordained priest in 1578, soon after his uncle's death. He was appointed Archbishop of Milan in 1595. He was a fine preacher. During the plague of 1627-28 in Milan he devoted all his efforts to relieving the famine in the city. He is shown in an heroic light in Alessandro Manzoni's great novel, *I Promessi Sposi*. In 1609 he founded the Ambrosian Library in Milan.

Champolion, J. F. (1790-1832) French writer on Egyptian archaeology. In 1828 he went with other scholars, at the expense of Charles X, to Egypt on an expedition where many important discoveries were made. His numerous works include *Précis du Système Hiéroglyphique des Anciens Egytiens*, and *Panthéon Egyptien*.

Consalvi, Cardinal Ercole (1757-1824) was born and died in Rome. His family, the Brunacci, were nobles of Pisa. His grandfather inherited a large fortune on the condition that he took the arms and name of Consalvi. His early education was with the Brothers of Pious Schools in Urbino. From 1771-76 he was at the Seminary in Frascati where he came to the attention of the Bishop of Frascati, Cardinal Henry Stuart of York (also known as Henry IX of England). He studied Law and Ecclesiastical History at the Accademia Ecclesiastica in Rome, and then entered the Administrative service of the Papal States. Consalvi was Assessor of the Military Commission when a French General, Duplot, was killed in Rome during the French occupation. Consalvi was arrested and imprisoned at the fortress of Sant' Angelo, but later allowed to go into exile in Naples. He sought to rejoin the exiled Pope Pius VI, but when this was disallowed he went to Venice. When the conclave to elect the successor to Pius VI was held in Venice in 1799 Consalvi was the unanimous choice as its Secretary. Pius VII, on his election, appointed Consalvi as Secretary of State in due course. A number of reforms within the Papal States were at his instigation. He firmly resisted pressure from Napoleon during the negotiations leading to the Concordat of 1801 with the French Government on the nature of the restoration of the Catholic religion in France. He advised Pius VII to agree to crown Napoleon Emperor, but resisted the Emperor's proposals to make the Pope the vassal of the Emperor. Napoleon, highly displeased at this, engineered Consalvi's dismissal as Secretary of State in retaliation. Consalvi then went to Paris and lived there in retirement, refusing a French Government pension. He subsequently declined to assist at the marriage of the Emperor with Maire Louise of Austria, after Napoleon had divorced Josephine. For this Napoleon sent him to Rheims where he lived in confinement. After Napoleon's downfall Consalvi rejoined the Pope in Italy who restored to him his position as Secretary of State. He subsequently played a key role at the Congress of Vienna in ensuring that the Papacy regained its temporal heritage. On his return to Rome Conslavi continued his domestic reform programme and promoted public works and the arts. Diplomatic agreements were concluded with Bavaria, Prussia, Hanover, Sardinia and the Two Sicilies. Wiseman's *Pius VII* describes the troubled relationship with Leo XII before the latter became Pope, and their eventual reconciliation before the Cardinal's death.

Cornelius, Peter von (1787-1866). A self taught painter, he went to Rome in 1811 and was a member of the Nazarene group of artists which sought to put art at the service of religion, and to revive the mediaeval Gothic style. Other members included Overbeck, Veit and the Schadow brothers. His work was acquired by the Prussian Consul General, and by museums in Dusseldorf and Munich. Later he became a celebrated teacher and administrator in Munich and was a leader of what came to be known as the Munich school.

Cretineau-Joly, Jacques (1803-1875). Journalist and historian. He was born at Fontenay-le-Conte in the Vendée in France. As a native of this famously Catholic and royalist region he wrote a sympathetic history of the Catholic and

Royalist uprising which took place there during the French revolution. His most famous work was a six volume history of the Jesuit Order published between 1844 and 1846, which demonstrated the author's unwavering fidelity to the Catholic Faith.

Cullen, Cardinal Paul (1803-1878) was born in Prospect, Kildare, Ireland. He studied at Propaganda Fide in Rome, was ordained in 1828, and went on to teach Scripture and Hebrew at Propaganda. He was Rector of the Irish College in Rome from 1832-1850, and for part of this time was also concurrently Rector of Propaganda. He was made Archbishop of Armagh in 1852, and transferred to Dublin in 1852. He was made the first Irish Cardinal Priest in 1857. He was a supporter of the Catholic University of Ireland project, and edited the *Acta* of the Congregation of Propaganda

Dalla Somaglia, Cardinal Giulio Maria (1744-1830) was born in Piacenza. He was ordained priest in 1787 and made Secretary of the Congregation of Bishops and Regulars of the Roman Curia. He was made a Bishop himself in 1800 and Prefect of the Congregation of Rites. In 1814 he became Secretary of the Roman Curia and Cardinal Bishop of Frascati. He was Archivist and Librarian of the Vatican from 1827 till his death.

D'Azeglio, Massimo (1798-1866). Painter, poet and political activist. Born of an aristocratic family in Turin, he went as a child into exile with his parents during the French occupation of Piedmont. In his youth he had sympathy for the *carbonari* and the revolutionary movements for change in Italy. But later he became critical of some of the results of change as they occurred. Despite his opposition to Gregory XVI's policies, he later favoured Papal rule over Rome, but not the return of its rule for the rest of the Papal States.

De Gregorio, Cardinal Emmanuele (1758-1839) was born at sea. He was made a Cardinal in 1816 and Prefect of the Roman Curia in 1818, and then promoted to be Prefect of the Council of the Curia in 1820. He became Bishop of Frascati in 1829, and Secretary of the Roman Curia in 1834.

Drovetti, Bernardino (1776-1852) was born in Turin. From 1803-1830 he was French Consul in Egypt where he played an important part in encouraging the reforms of Pasha Mohammed Ali. His large collection of Egyptian artifacts was bequeathed to various Italian museums.

Fornari, Cardinal Rafaele (1787-1854) was born in Rome. His ecclesiastical career came into prominence when he was appointed Bishop of Nicaea in 1842. In 1843 he was sent as Nuncio to Paris. In 1846 he was made Cardinal *in pectore* and publicly proclaimed Cardinal Priest of S. Maria sopra Minerva in 1850. In 1849, the Council of Spoleto had asked the Pope for a collective condemnation of current modern errors deemed inconsistent with the Faith. Three years later, Fornari, on the order of Pius IX, wrote to a number of bishops and lay people for assistance in the study of prevalent errors. A draft syllabus of these was prepared and underwent various manifestations, and was even proclaimed by some bishops. Finally, in 1864, on the anniversary of the Feast of the Immaculate Conception, Cardinal Antonelli formally sent to all bishops the document known as The Syllabus of Errors.

Giustiniani, Cardinal Giacomo (1769-1843) was born in Rome, was ordained priest in 1816, and soon after was made apostolic nuncio to Spain in 1817 by Pius VII. He was appointed Cardinal Priest of Ss Marcellino e Pietro in 1826. According to Wiseman, although he achieved the most votes in preliminary voting at the conclave of 1831, he was blocked from the papacy by Ferdinand VII of Spain. He resigned as Cardinal Priest of Ss Marcellino e Pietro in

1832. He was appointed Prefect of the Roman Curia in 1834 and Cardinal Bishop of Albano in 1839. He became Protector of the Venerable English College after the death of Cardinal Weld. He was the uncle of Cardinal Odescalchi.

Havercamp, Sigebert (1683-1742). A celebrated Dutch scholar he was born in Leyden. While travelling in Italy he developed an interest in medals and coins, and subsequently published a work on numismatics. As Professor of Greek, History and Rhetoric at the University of Leyden he produced critical editions of Josephus, Tertullian, Lucretius, Juvenal, Orosius, Sallust and Censorinus.

Hermes, Georg (1794-1876). Philosopher and theologian. He was born in Dreierwalde, Westphalia and was educated at the University of Münster where he was influenced by the ideas of Kant. He was ordained priest in 1799. The success of his early writings led to his being appointed Professor of Dogmatic Theology at Münster in 1807. He moved to a chair at Bonn on the creation of a University there. However, when his writings were examined in detail by the Jesuit Fr Giovanni Perrone* (see below), in the light of concerns expressed by some of the German bishops, his work was condemned in Gregory XVI's brief *Dum acerbissimum* of 26 September 1835. The core of the charge against Hermes' wrtings was their implicit rationalism. When Doste zu Vishering became Archbishop of Cologne he required all candidates for the priesthood to subscribe to 18 anti-Hermesian propositions. Most Hermesians in due course came to accept the ruling of the Papal Brief.

Hyrcanus, John. Jewish Maccabean ruler who reigned from 134 to 104 BC. He was a nephew of Judas Maccabeus. He was the last of the Jewish rulers to combine successfully the office of King and High Priest.

Lambruschini, Cardinal Luigi (1776-1854) was born at Sestri Levante, and later entered the Barnabite Congregation. He was Secretary to Cardinal Consalvi at the Congress of Vienna. In 1815 he became Secretary of the Congregation for Extraordinary Affairs. He was made Archbishop of Genoa in 1819. Leo XII sent him as his nuncio to Paris in 1827. In 1831 he was made a Cardinal by Gregory XVI, and became his Secretary of State in 1836. He received a majority in the first ballot at the Papal election in 1846, but was not elected. He resigned as Secretary of State after the conclave because he was out of sympathy with Pius IX's constitutional policies, but continued as Cardinal Librarian until his death.

Lamennais, Félicité de (1782-1854) Born at St Malo, he was ordained priest in 1816. He published his first work *Essai sur l'indifference en matière de religion* a few years after his ordination. He began the journal *L'Avenir* with the epigraph 'God and Liberty' in September 1830. When it was condemned by the Pope in 1832 by the encyclical *Mirari vos* he closed it. But he then went on to publish a speculative and apocalyptic work, *Paroles d'un croyant* on 30 April 1834. This in its turn was condemned by the Encyclical *Singulari nos*. He was imprisoned in 1840 for a breach of the French press laws. He translated Dante in his later years, and died in Paris unreconciled to the Church.

Liguori, St Alphonsus Mary (1696-1787). Bishop and Doctor of the Church. He was born in Marianella near Naples where his father owned a villa. He trained as a lawyer and became a successful barrister. He was ordained priest in 1726. He founded the Congregation of the Most Holy Redeemer, for the special intention of mission work among farmers and agricultural workers. When the congregation received papal approval he was elected Superior General in 1749. In 1762, against his wishes he was appointed Bishop of Sant'Agata dei Goti by Clement XIII.

He suffered many subsequent trials when his congregation was riven with internal divisions. He is famous for his work of Moral Theology. He was an opponent of Jansenism, and his work, *The Glories of Mary* (1750) defended Marianism. He was canonised on Trinity Sunday 1839, on the same day as Father Francis Jerome S.J. to whom his mother had presented him soon after his birth. He was made a Doctor of the Church by Leo XIII in 1879.

Litta, Cardinal Lorenzo (1756-1820). Born of a noble Milanese family he was ordained priest in 1789, and made a bishop in 1793. He was sent as a Papal nuncio to Warsaw in 1794, and later was legate to the Russian Federation at St Petersburg. He persuaded Tsar Paul I to restore the Basilian religious order and the church property confiscated by Catherine II, and he reorganised the Russian dioceses of the Latin rite. In 1799, however, he was forced to leave Russia. He became Treasurer of the Papal States and was made a Cardinal by Pius VII in 1801. He was expelled from Rome by Napoleon I for loyalty to Pius VII. He refused to attend the Emperor's second wedding to Marie-Louise of Austria. On his return to Rome in 1814 he was appointed Prefect of Propaganda, and in 1818 became Cardinal Vicar of Rome.

Loisy, Alfred (1857-1940). French theologian and scripture scholar. He was ordained priest in 1879, and was Professor at the Catholic Institute in Paris from 1881 to 1893. He was critical of the literal interpretation of the biblical accounts of creation, and argued that biblical criticism could be applied to the Church's interpretation of scripture, and for greater freedom for scholars to interpret the history and development of religious doctrine. His writings were collectively condemned by the Church, and a number were specifically criticised. He was dismissed from the Catholic Institute in 1893 and excommunicated in 1908. His later writings seem to be aimed at developing a kind of liberal humanitarianism. His autobiography appeared in 1924.

BIOGRAPHICAL SKETCHES 87

Marco, Cardinal Juan Francisco y Catalán (1771-1841). He was elevated to the Cardinalate in 1828 by Leo XII and became Cardinal Deacon of S. Agata dei Goti. Ferdinand VII of Spain entrusted him with the delicate task of conveying to the 1831 conclave Spain's veto of Cardinal Giustiniani, the fomer Papal nuncio in Madrid, as a candiate for the papacy.

Mezzofanti, Cardinal Giuseppe (1774-1849). Born in Bologna, he studied Oriental languages before being ordained in 1797. He was appointed to the chair of Hebrew at the University of Bologna. After refusing to take the oath to the Cisalpine Republic he was dismissed from his chair, but undertook other academic and librarian appointments in the University. With the restoration of Papal rule he was made Professor of Oriental Languages in 1815. After the revolutionary upheaval in Bologna he was part of a delegation which went to Rome in 1831 to apologise to Pius VIII on behalf of the citizens of that city. In 1833 he was made Custodian of the Vatican Library, and Prefect of the Congregation of Oriental Rites. He was made a Cardinal in 1839. He is widely reported as being able to speak 38 languages fluently, and to know about 30 others.

Mozzi, Fr Luigi (1746-1813). He became a Jesuit in 1763. When the order was suppressed in 1773 he was made a Canon of Bergamo, and examined candidates for the priesthood in that diocese. He rejoined the Jesuits when the congregation was re-established, and from 1804 was based in Naples. Pius VI appointed him an apostolic missioner with special responsibility to counter Jansenism.

Niebuhr, Berthold Georg (1776-1831). He was born in Copenhagen, the son of a celebrated Danish traveller. At the age of nineteen he went to Edinburgh to study the natural sciences. He followed this with a tour of England to become familiar with its institutions. In 1806 he entered the service of the King of Prussia, becoming a Privy Counsellor and working in the Department of Finance. When the University of Berlin was founded in 1810 his friends persuaded him to lecture on the history of Rome in which he had an interest. In 1811/12 he published his two volume *History of Rome* in which he cast doubt on some earlier historians' factual claims.

Odescalchi, Cardinal Carlo (1786-1841). Born in Rome, he spent his early years as a member of the household of Pius VII. He was a nephew of Cardinal Giustiniani. In 1823 he was made cardinal Archbishop of Ferrara. He resigned his see in 1826 and returned to Rome where he was appointed bishop of Sabia and Prefect of several congregations. He resigned his cardinalate in 1839 in order to become a Jesuit.

Overbeck, Johann Friedrich (1789-1869). German painter and convert to Catholicism. After 1910 he lived almost entirely in Rome as the most important member of the Nazarene group, which he founded with Pforr. The school sought to make art serve religion. He idolized Raphael and painted almost entirely in a Quattrocento style. His work is in Santa Maria degli Angeli at Assisi, at Cologne Cathedral, and in Munich, Berlin and elsewhere.

Pacca, Cardinal Bartolomeo (1756-1844). Born in Benevento, he studied in Rome. Pius VI appointed him Papal Nuncio in Cologne and later in Lisbon. In 1801 he was created Cardinal. In 1808 he succeeded Cardinal Consalvi as pro-Secretary of State, and was kidnapped with Pius VII by Napoleon's troops. He was imprisoned at Fenestrelle, then deported to Uzès. In 1814 he returned with Pius VII to Rome. The strong line he took against Napoleon at the Congress of Vienna brought to an end his diplomatic career. He was given various administrative appointments by Leo XII, including that of Cardinal legate at Velletri. He

BIOGRAPHICAL SKETCHES

vigorously opposed the *carbonari*. He was a noted patron of the arts and financed the excavations at Ostia.

Perrone, Giovanni (1794-1876). Theologian. Born at Chieri (Turin), he entered the Society of Jesus in 1815. A few years later he began teaching dogmatic theology, first at Orvieto, then at the Collegeo Romano. After the revolutionary agitation of 1848 he spent three years teaching theology at the Jesuit Scholasticate at Benbank in Wales. He returned to the Collegio Romano in 1851. From 1853 until his death he acted either as Rector or Prefect of Studies at the College. He played a key role in the theological struggle against the influence of the ideas of Georg Hermes*(see above), and also laid the groundwork for the definition of the dogma of the Immaculate Conception and of Papal Infallibility. He was well-grounded in patristics and wrote clearly and concisely.

Schadow, Friedrich Wilhelm (1789-1862). He was a son of Johann Gottfried Schadow, court sculptor in Berlin, and himself became an artist, art historian, teacher and arts administrator. He went to Rome in 1810 with his brother Rudolph. They both converted to Catholicism and became part of the Nazarene school. On his return to Germany he became Head of the Art schools in Berlin and Dusseldorf where his reputation attracted many scholars and artists.

Schadow, Rudolph. Sculptor and younger brother of Friedrich Schadow. He studied with Antonio Canova and with Bertil Thorwaldsen, the Danish sculptor who spent many years in Rome. Schadow's work is in the neo-classical style. A major sculptural piece of his is the tomb of Pius VII.

Severoli, Cardinal Antonio Gabriele (1757-1824). Born in Faenza, he was ordained priest in 1779. Pius VI made him bishop of Fano in 1787. He was appointed Apostolic Nuncio to Austria in 1801, and archbishop of Viterbo and Tuscania in 1808. In 1816, after Pius VII's restoration, he was made Cardinal Priest of S Maria in Pace in Rome. According to Wiseman Austria vetoed him as a possible pope at the conclave of 1823.

Theiner, Fr Augustin (1804-1874). This Catholic historian was born in Breslau. As a priest he entered the Congregazione dell' Oratorio. In 1855 he was appointed Prefect of the Vatican archives. He was a well-known figure in Rome to such long term residents as the pianist and composer Franz Liszt. Newman and Theiner exchanged letters and gifts of books, and it was the latter who encouraged Newman and his friends to become Oratorians. He also tried unsuccesfully to persuade them to run an Oratory in Malta. Fr Theiner was also involved in the Achilli affair, and was sent by Pius IX to try to reconcile this ex-Dominican with the Church. Newman esteemed Theiner as the only real scholar and decent preacher in the Roman Oratory at that time. During the First Vatican Council (1869-70) Theiner was dismissed from his archive office for leaking sensitive documents to opponents of the declaration of papal infallibility (eg Cardinal Hohenlowe). With the advent of secular government the religious communities, including the Oratorians in Rome were dispersed. Later, as he lay dying, Theiner's servant and landlady telegraphed Pius IX to obtain absolution for him. This came, together with the Pope's special benediction. He was buried in the German Cemetery in Rome.

Tosti, Cardinal Angelo (1776-1866) was born in Rome. As Gregory XVI's Treasurer he was responsible for arranging the finance for the restoration of the Lateran Palace. He was made a Cardinal *in pectore* in 1838, and publicly proclaimed in 1839. He became Vatican Librarian in 1860.

Veit, Philip (1783-1878). Painter and member of the Nazarene school in Rome. His mother was the daughter of the composer

Felix Mendelsohn, and his wife the daughter of Friedrich Schlegel, the celebrated German critic and philologist. In later years he painted in Frankfurt.

Weld, Cardinal Thomas (1773-1837) was born in London and educated privately by a Jesuit priest to whose Society he later gave hospitality at his property at Stonyhurst. He married Lady Bridget Clifford at Ugbroke in 1796. They had a daughter Mary Lucy, who married her cousin, Hugh, 7th Baron Clifford of Chudleigh who was related to Cardinal Giacomo Giustiniani (see above). After the death of his wife he studied for the priesthood and was ordained in 1821. He became Co-adjutor Bishop of Kingston Ontario, Canada in 1826, but never visited his diocese, in part because of his concern about his daughter's health. After Catholic Emancipation he was appointed in the following year (1830), Cardinal Priest of S. Marcello, and so participated at the Papal Conclave of 1831 at which Gregory XVI was elected. When in Rome Cardinal Weld lived at the Palazzo Odescalchi where he received the British and Roman aristocracy, and followed events and affairs in the English-speaking world. He was Protector of the Venerable English College after the death of Cardinal Zurla in 1834.

Zurla, Cardinal Giacinto Placido (1769-1834) was born in Legnano. At the age of eighteen he joined the Camaldolese Order at San Michaele di Murano in Venice. In 1809 he was elected Definitor of his Congregation. In 1821 he went to Rome and became Prefect of Studies at the Collegio Urbano. In 1823 he was made Cardinal. He was Cardinal Vicar to Popes Leo XII, Pius VIII and Gregory XVI. He published a book about Marco Polo, and was particularly interested in ancient maps. He succeeded Cardinal Consalvi as Protector of the Venerable English College and held this office until his death.

ANNEX B

It is the desire of the Cardinal Archbishop and of the Archbishops of England and Wales that public as well as private prayer and intercession be constantly offered up to God for the conversion of our country. It was determined by a resolution, dated May 2nd, 1867, that Exposition and Benediction of the Blessed Sacrament on the Second Sunday of every month should be for this intention. The following prayers, composed by his Eminence Cardinal Wiseman may be said on this and other occasions, even during the Exposition of the Blessed Sacrament.

PRAYERS FOR THE CONVERSION OF ENGLAND AND WALES

TO BEG THE PRAYERS OF THE SAINTS

O MERCIFUL GOD,
let the glorious intercession of thy saints assist us;
above all, the most blessed Virgin Mary,
Mother of thy holy Apostles, Peter and Paul,
to whose patronage we humbly recommend this our land.
Be mindful of our fathers, Eleutherius, Celestine and Gregory,
bishops of the holy City;
of Augustine, Columba, and Aidan,
who delivered to us inviolate
the faith of the holy Roman Church.
Remember all those holy confessors, bishops and kings,
all those holy monks and hermits,
all those holy widows and virgins,
who made this once an island of saints,

illustrious by their glorious merits and virtues.
Let not their memory perish from before thee, O Lord,
but let their supplications enter daily into thy sight;
and do thou, who didst so often spare thy sinful people
for the sake of Abraham, Isaac, and Jacob, now, also,
moved by the prayers of our fathers reigning with thee,
have mercy upon us, save thy people,
and bless thine inheritance;
and suffer not those souls to perish,
which thy Son hath redeemed
with his own most precious blood.
Who liveth and reigneth with Thee, world without end.

Let us pray.

O LOVING LORD Jesu,
who, when thou wert hanging on the Cross,
didst commend us all, in the person of thy disciple John,
to thy most sweet Mother,
that we might find in her our refuge, our solace and our hope;
look graciously upon our beloved land,
and on those who are bereaved of so powerful a patronage;
that, acknowledging once more the dignity of this holy Virgin,
that they may honour and venerate her
with all affection of devotion,
and own her as Queen and Mother.
May her sweet name be lisped by little ones,
and linger on the lips of the aged and the dying;
and may it be invoked by the afflicted,
and hymned by the joyful;
that this Star of the Sea being their protection and guide,
all may come to the harbour of eternal salvation.
Who livest and reignest, world without end.

R. Amen.

ANNEX C

THE PAPAL ENCYCLICALS OF GREGORY XVI

1. **Summo Iugiter Studio** (1832—on mixed marriages)

2. **Cum Primum** (1832—on civil obedience).

3. **Mirari Vos** (1832—on errors of political and religious liberalism and indifferentism, and on abuses of freedom).

4. **Quo Graviora** (1833—on rights of the Church and Church discipline).

5. **Singulari Nos** (1834—on the writings and ideas of Lamennais).

6. **Commissum Divinitus** (1835—on Church and State).

7. **In Supremo Apostolatus Fastigio** (1839—in condemnation of the slave trade).

8. **Probe Nostis** (1840—on the propagation of the Faith).

9. **Quo Vestro** (1841—on mixed marriages).

10. **Inter Praecipuas** (1844—on biblical societies).

INDEX

Abyssinia *ix*
Academia of Cortona,
    transactions of 15
Acton, Elizabeth, married to Sir Robert
    Throckmorton 40
ACTON, CARDINAL CHARLES
    birth 39
    early education in England 39
    attends Magdalene College,
        Cambridge 39
    attends *Academia Ecclesiastica*
        in Rome 40
    made papal chamberlain
        by Leo XII 40
    attaché in Paris 40
    Vice-legate in Bologna 40
    marries sister to
        Sir Robert Throckmorton 40
    assistant judge of Civil Court
        in Rome 40
    friend of Père Géramb 36
    Auditor of the Apostolic Chamber
        in Rome 40
    made Cardinal *in petto* 41
    proclaimed Cardinal and Member
        of the Sacred College 41
    records that Gregory XVI sometimes
        overturned recommendations
        of Papal Congregations 59
    only witness at conference
        between Gregory XVI and
        Emperor of Russia 41-2, 62
    refuses bishopric in Naples offered
        by King of Naples 42
    clarity of prose praised by
        Gregory XVI 41
    musical powers and wit 41
    intimate friend of Amelia, wife of
        King Louis Philippe of France 42
    large personal charities result in need
        for personal austerity 42
    death in Palermo 41
Acton, Sir Ferdinand, older brother of
    Cardinal Acton 41
Acton, Sir John Francis Edward,
    father of Sir Francis and
    Cardinal Acton 39
Ædes Lateranae, see Lateran Palace

Agricola, Professor 2
Ahmed Fethis Pasha, Ottoman
    ambassador in Paris 29
Aix-la-Chapelle 50
Albani, Cardinal Giuseppe
    Secretary of State to Pius VIII
Albano 36, 49
    lake of *viii*
Aldenham, Salop 41
Alertz, Dr 58
Alexander the Great, manuscript
    of itineraries of 46
Alexander II, Emperor of Russia
    as Czarowich visits Rome 61
Altieri, Prince later Cardinal 9, 52
Ambrosian Library in Milan 43-6, 52
America, North *ix*
Anabises 20
Ancona, severity of cholera outbreak
    at 68
Anio River 12
Antinous, statue of 22
Antoninus Pius, letters of Emperor 46
Antonelli, Cardinal Giacomo 22, 70
Appian, letters of 46
Apostolic vicars of England 30
Appartamento Borgia in Vatican 20
Arabic 48
Archaeology 15-20, 26, 28-9
Arco della Badia 16
Arianism 70
Aristides, statue of 22
Armenian 48
Asia 24
Assisi 67
Assyrian monuments 15
Augustus, Emperor 43
Aurelius Symmacchus, speeches of 46
Ausonius, Decimus Magnus, 56, 56.1
Austria *ix*

Bailey, Canon John *acknowledgments*
banditti 5
Baronius, Cardinal Cesare 34
Beaumont, Rev M
    gives first Holy Communion to
        future Cardinal Acton 39
Belluno, birthplace of Gregory XVI i, 4

Belvedere Court in Vatican 20-22
Belzoni, Giovanni Battista 18
Benedict XIV, pioneer of
   papal encyclicals xi
Benzoni, Giovan Maria, sculptor 52
Bergamo, episcopal seminary at 43
Berlin 33
Bessarion, Basilius 47
Blake, Rev Dr Michael Bishop of
   Dromore, student & Rector of
   the Irish College 69-70
Bobbio, monastery of 44
Bologna 40
   renews fealty to the Pope 37
   birthplace of Br Ferri 67
Bonaparte, Prince Lucien 16
Borghese, Princess Gwendolen,
   charitable work in Rome of 28
Borromeo, Cardinal Frederico 44
Borromeo, Charles
   (see St Charles Borromeo)
Bourbons x
Boylan, Rev Dr 69
Bow Street police station in London 35
Boxing, mosaic of ancient Roman 22-3
Bradford 24
Braschi Palace 22
brevier 45
British Museum 16
Bunsen, Chevalier 34
Byrne, Very Rev Robert
   acknowledgments
Byzantine paintings,
   Gregory XVI's bequest of 21

Caelean Hill 5
California 38
Camaldolese Order i, xx, 4-7, 7.1
   monastic and eremitical forms of 5
Campania 15
Canada 60
Cannino 16
Canonisations 39
Canopus, large Egyptian jar 19. 19.4
Capital Museum in Rome 22
Cappellari, Bartolomeo Alberto (see
   Gregory XVI)
carbonari xx, xx.1

Cardinalate, regulars preserve colour of
   monastic habits when elevated to
   the 4, 4.1, 6-7
"Cardinal *in pectore*," cardinal made
   but not publicly proclaimed 7
Castel-Gandolfo, Franciscan
   monastery of 35-6
Catholic temporal Powers, influence
   on Papal election of 1-3
*Catholic Thought since the
   Enlightenment* xvii
"chemin d'infer" vii
Cerae 16
cestus, boxer's glove 26
Chambers of Commerce in Papal
   States 12
Champollion, J.F 19, 19.2
Charles X of France x
Charon, ferryman of dead
   in Greek myth 16, 16.1
Chiusi 15
Cholera outbreak of 1837 xii, 26-8
   sanitary measures at Monte Porzio 27-8
   number of deaths in Rome from 28
   excellence of medical statistics on 28
Christ, Our Lord Jesus, invoked
   by Cardinal Mai in
   sepulchral inscription 53
Christian Museum in the Vatican 21
   enriched by Gregory XVI 21
Christian painting in Rome,
   19th century German school of 33-4
Cicero, Marcus Tullus 46-8
   discovery of his "*De Republica*" 47
Cistercian Order, La Trappe
   branch of 36-7
Civic Guard in Rome 9
*Classici Scriptores ex codicibus
   Vaticanis editi* by Cardinal Mai 49
Clement VIII, water-organ in the
   Quirinal Palace of; restored
   by Gregory XVI *viii*
Clement XIV 7
Code of Procedure in Papal States 12
Codex Vaticanus 48
Cologne, archbishop of 61
Columbus, Christopher 6
Colombanus, (See St Columbanus)

INDEX

Colorno 43
Commonplace Book of Monsignor Alfred Gilbey xviii.1
Conclave of 1831 1-4
Congregation of Propaganda ix, 48, 59, 68-9, 73
Consalvi, Cardinal Hercule
   with Cardinal Litta selects
     Cardinal Mai as Vatican
     Librarian 46
Constantine, Roman Emperor 23, 46
Constantius Augustus 46
converts xv.1, 68
Cornelius, Peter von 33
Cortona (see also Academia of Cortona Transactions) 15
Corvettes and the slave trade 29
Council of Trent 34
"Court Guide", Roman 38
Crawford, F. Marion xv, xv.1, xv.3
   prediction of future disastrous
     Italian military adventures xv.1-2
Cretineau-Joly, Jacques vii, xx
Cullen, Cardinal Paul 69
Cynocephali 20

Dalla Somaglia, Cardinal Giulio 40
Dante 33
David, King of Israel, tomb of 16.2
D'Azeglio, Massimo vi-vii
De Bouteneff, Russian Minister at Rome 62
De facto governments,
   papal attitude to x
De Gregorio, Cardinal Emmanuele 37
De Lamennais (see Lamennais)
De Republica of Cicero 47
Demosthenes, manuscripts of 44
Diocletian, Emperor 66
Dionysius of Halicarnassus,
   history of 46
Divine Comedy 23
Dirce, Farnesian statue of 14
Dover 24
Dresden 20
Dromore 69
Drovetti, Bernardino 18
Dublin, archbishop of 69

Dublin Review 67.1
"Dunce of the College" 70
Düsseldorf 33-4

earthquakes in Umbria 66
Ecclesiastical History
   of Baronius 34
Egyptian artifacts, 15, 18-20
Egyptian hieroglyphics 19
Eleanor, novel by
   Mrs Humphrey Ward xv
Emperor of Austria (see Francis I)
Emperor of Russia (see Nicholas I)
England & Papal States
   compared 31-2
English College (see Venerable English College)
Ennius, Quintus 56, 56.2
Episcopal consecration of pope
   not yet a bishop 7
Epistola encyclica et commonitoria
   of Benedict XIV on duties
     of Episcopate xi
Esdras, Book of 52
Ethiopia (see Abyssinia)
Etruscan Museum 28
Etruscans 15-18, 20, 28
Eurysaces, Marcus Vergilius,
   tomb of wife of 29
Eusebius, two books of the
   Chronicles of 46

Fabiola, novel by Wiseman front.
Farnesi 14
Ferdinand I of Naples 43
Ferdinand II of Naples 42
Ferdinand VII of Spain 2-3
Ferri, Br Luigi 67
Flaminian Way 58
Florence 20
   Prussian Embassy at 58
Fornari, Professor,
   later Cardinal Rafaele 40
Fra Angelico, Beato 21
France 24
Francis I of Austria 2
Frankfurt, Christian school of
   Art at 33

Free medical provision in
　Papal States 27, 27.1
Freemasonry xix, xx
French Government:
　its occupation of Rome xiii
　seeks to prevent Austria from
　　aiding Gregory XVI
　　during insurrection 11.2
French monarchists xviii
French Revolution i, ix
Fronto, Marcus Cornelius
　letters of 46-7
funeral observances for
　Cardinals 38-9

Gallic acid (used to reveal
　palimpsests) 45
gas lighting in Rome xii
*Gentle Regrets: Thoughts
　on a Life* xix
George III of England 35
Géramb, Baron Ferdinand
　later Père 35-7
German artists in Rome 33-4
German scientific association
　in Rome 34
Germany 24
Gilbey, Monsignor Alfred xviii.1
Giustiniani, Cardinal Giacomo
　uncle of Cardinal Odelaschi 2
　blocked from papacy by Spain
　　for supporting Leo XII's
　　policy of providing bishops
　　to rebel Spanish colonies 1-2
　appears miserable when in
　　danger of becoming pope
　　at 1831 conclave 2
　moving speech at conclave
　　after being blocked for
　　papacy by Spain 3
Good Friday in Rome, muffled
　drums of xiv
Grand Tour
　Protestant liberals criticise
　　backwardness of Papal States on xiv
　tourists' sense of loss after
　　1870 xv and xv.2 &3
Greece 24

Greek 48, 50, 52
Gregory the Great (see St Gregory)
Gregory XV ix
GREGORY XVI
　Early years
　　born at Belluno near Venice
　　　on 8 September 1765 v, 4
　　family from minor nobility v, 4
　　decides on religious vocation
　　　at age of 18 xx, 4
　　enters Camaldolese order in
　　　1783 v, 4
　　named Mauro in religion v, 4
　　formative years at San Michele
　　　di Murano v, 4
　　ordained priest in 1787 v
　　teaches philosophy at San Michele v
　　publishes in 1799 *Il Trionfo della
　　　Santa Sede e della Chiesa contro gli
　　　assalti dei novatori combattuti e respinti
　　　colle stesse loro armi* vi, 4, 4.2
　　admirer of St Thomas Aquinas v
　　influence on Catholic theology
　　　and Dogma of Papal Infallibility vi
　Ecclesiastical appointments
　　serves in Holy Office at Venice v
　　established at Camaldolese Centre
　　　in Rome in 1795 5
　　created Cardinal *in petto* by
　　　Leo XII in 1825 7
　　prolaimed Cardinal in consistory in
　　　1826 with eulogy by Leo XII 7
　　Prefect of Propaganda Fide ix, 59, 73
　　chosen by Leo XII to negotiate with
　　　Spanish envoy on Holy See's
　　　decision to fill bishoprics in Spain's
　　　Latin American rebel colonies x
　Papacy
　　elected Pope on 2 February 1831 7
　　receives episcopal consecration
　　　before coronation 7
　　rumours of insurrection
　　　in Papal States on day of
　　　election 8
　　invites in Austrian troops to protect
　　　Papal States from revolution
　　　ix, 11, 11.2, 12
　　establishes sinking fund to repay

debt for Austrian intervention 12
enlarges the Civic Guard with
  Prince Altieri as commander 9
remains calm and active in face
  of insurrection 10
Roman poor show strong support
  for him as Pope 9
tour of the Papal States *xi*
Civil Administration and public
works
divides the Secretary of State's
  office into Home and Foreign
  Affairs departments 26
reorganises local government 12
revises Civil and Criminal
  Code of Law 12
establishes National Bank *xii*, 26
issues a new coinage with greater
  decimal features *xii*, 26
introduces Chambers of Commerce
  xii, 12
provides new system for
  Public Works Department 26
funds tunnels in the Anio River at
  Tivoli to prevent flooding 12, 26
restores the Roman Forum 26
has Monastery of St Gregory
  repaired at his own expense 26
large public works executed at
  mouth of the Tiber and
  Cività Vecchia 26
finishes new public cemetery at
  Basilica of St Lawrence and
  prohibits intramural burial 26
consecrates re-built Basilica of
  St Paul fuori le Mura *xi*
Cultural initiatives
founds first Etruscan and Egyptian
  museums in the Vatican *viii*, 18
gives own rare valuable Byzantine
  paintings to Vatican Museum 21
arranges for the preservation of
  frescoes in Vatican previously
  open to elements 21
founds new Christian museum in
  Lateran Palace 23
restores water organ which
  Clement VIII had placed in

Quirinal Palace *viii*
personal enthusiasm for opera *viii*
Missionary activity
promotes foreign missions as
  Propaganda-Prefect and Pope *ix*
opens missions in Abyssinia, India,
  China, among North American
  natives, and in Polynesia *ix*
supports Leo XII's policy of
  providing bishops to Spanish rebel
  colonies in Latin America *x*
acquainted with affairs of British
  dominions 65
increases the number of Apostolic
  Vicariates in England 68
appoints Wiseman co-adjutor
  bishop in Midlands 30-1
predicts to Wiseman restoration
  of English hierarchy 68
Foreign policy
recognises government of
  King Louis Philippe *x*
Bull *Sollicitudo Ecclesiarum* confirms
  traditional papal policy of
  recognising *de facto* regimes 13
forcibly rebukes Emperor of Russia
  for treatment of Catholic
  subjects 62-4
encyclical *In Supremo Apostolatus
  fastigio* condemns slavery and
  slave trade 29
Religious policy
retains traditional liturgical and
  civil ceremonies *xii*
provides for the splendour of divine
  worship but wears nothing
  costly himself 59
prepared to interrupt Papal
  processions to talk to children *viii*
develops papal encyclicals on
  pressing issues *xi*, 60
encyclical *Mirari Vos* rejects
  many aspects of liberalism *xi*
encyclical *Singulari Nos* condemns
  writings of Lamennais *xi*, 65
walks in procession to invoke mercy
  of God during cholera epidemic 27
canonises St Alphnsus Liguori and

others 30
commissions history of freemasonry
  and secret societies, but not
  published xix-xx
Public health and natural disasters
  Personal efforts to stamp
    out cholera *xii*, 26-7
  establishes Sanitary Commission
    for 1837 cholera epidemic and
    supernumerary hospitals 26-8
  subscribes personally to fund to
    educate plague orphans 28
  refuses to appoint personal Papal
    doctor to conserve papal funds 58
  provides state relief for victims of
    1833-4 earthquakes in Umbria 67
Death
  dies on 1 June 1846 *xx*
  widely mourned: Romans queue
    to kiss his feet at St Peter's
    Basilica *xx*
  but lampooned on death by poet
    and statesman D'Azeglio *vi-vii*
  many philsophical judgements
    posthumously vindicated *xvi-xix*
Physical characteristics
  face large and rounded
    without fine features 57
  expression lights up when
    discussing grave topics 58
  eyes bright and animated
    in conversation 58
  robust health 58-9
  first pope to be photographed
    xi, *xi.2*
  cancerous growth on face
    successfully removed 58
Personal characteristics
  paternal instinct towards
    children *viii*, 66
  sense of humour *vii-viii*
  lack of self-importance *vii*
  quixotic nature *xiii*, *xx*
  amiability and simplicity
    of character according to
    Wiseman 59
  conservative in temperament *viii*
  firmness of resolve 65

goodhearted but obstinate and
  narrow according to *The Oxford
  Dictionary of Popes* *vi*
known to many Englishmen on
  Grand Tour visiting Rome 57
impresses Englishwoman seeking
  to upbraid him for claiming
  infallibility charism *vii*
daily walks 58
favourite walk in Rome
  on Flaminian Way 58
love of touring in Castelli Romani
  viii
love of water *v*
love of water games in
  Quirinal Palace *viii*
love of fishing *viii*
provides French sweets to his
  Cardinals *viii*
only discourses freely in Latin
  and Italian 57
drafts well in Latin 60
agrees to proof read Wiseman's
  essay 1
acquainted with poetry and able
  to discuss it 58
unwearying assiduity &
  cheerfulness in conducting
  public business 59
carefully considers all state papers
  and not uncommonly
  rejects Congregations'
  recommendations 59
hatred of railways *vi*, *xii*, 31
opposed to gas lighting as against
  Roman popular *mores* *xii*
extensive personal charities 66
fine personal library and
  art collection 75
interest in English art 75
leans on the side of mercy in
  capital sentences 60
unimpressed by the strength
  and pride of opponents 60-1
overturns Canadian bishop's
  advice and is vindicated 60
rises very early; chaplain not
  required to assist at own early

INDEX

Mass 59
  prone to tears during prayer 64
  claims Holy Spirit guided conduct
    of meeting with Russian
    Emperor 63
  personal kindness to Wiseman
    75-6
Guido, Signor 20

Hadrian (also Adrian),
  Emperor 19, 19.3
Halicarnassus 14
Hare, Augustus xv, xv.i
Havercamp, Sigebert 17.1
Health Service in Papal States
  free medicine in all Papal
    communes 27, 27.1
Hebrew 20, 43, 52
Hecules, Farnesian statue of 14
Hermes, Georg 65
Herod of Israel, King 17.1
Hesse-Homberg of Reuss 25
Hierarchical society, value of xviii.1
Holy Office v
Holy Year of 1825 xiv
Homer, manuscript of 44
Horace, Quintus Flaccus 11, 11.1
Hyrcanus 17.1

*Il trionfo della Santa Sede e della Chiesa
  contro gli assalti dei innovatori* vi, 4.3
*Imperial City: Rome, Romans and
  Napoleon* xiii.1
India ix
Inferno of Dante 33
In supremo apostolatus fastigio,
  Bull against the slave trade x.2, 29
Insurance company in Papal States for
  fire and hail 28
In vita Agathiae 56.2
Irish College in Rome 69-70
Isleworth 39
Italian, free discourse of
  Gregory XVI in 57
Italian Hours, travel book of
  Henry James xi
Italy, invasion by the French of v

Jacob, Rev Dominic *acknowledgments*
James, Henry xi
James II of England 30
Jesuits (see Society of Jesus)
Jesuit house at Tivoli xi
Jones, Rev Mr, tutor to future
  Cardinal Acton 39
Josephus, Flavius 17.1
Julius Valerius, three books on
  Alexander the Great of 46

Kelly, J.N.D., editor of
  The Oxford Dictionary of Popes vi.1
Kestner, Baron, Prussian Ambassador
  to Papal States 57

Labrador, Spanish Ambassador to
  Holy See at conclave of 1831-2, 12
La Divina Commedia 33
Lambruschini, Cardinal Luigi,
  Chief Vatican Librarian
  before Cardinal Mai 49
Lambruschini, Giovanni Battista,
  Bishop of Orvieto 43
Lamennais, Félicité Robert de
  calls for freepress xvi
  publishes *Paroles d'un croyant*
    in 1834 xix, 65
  Paroles condemned by Pope
    in *Singulari nos* xix, 65
  papal condemnation foreshadows
    censure of Modernism xvi
  defends religion not through reason,
    but as arising from the
    sens commun of the faithful xvii
  sees role for pope as universal pastor;
    sort of ultramontanist xvii
  supporter of democracy and
    liberty xvi
  his mystical *sens commun*
    could make populace prey
    to charismatic leaders xviii-xix
  dies unreconciled to the Church
    in 1840 xvi
Lateran Palace, 23, 33
  Egyptian obelisk before 18
Latin 48, 52
  free discourse of Gregory XVI in 57

La Trappe, monastery of 37
Leeds 30
LEO XII *ix*, 4, 6-7, 12, 69, 75
Litta, Cardinal Lorenzo 46
London 14, 20
Loisy, Alfred *xvi*
Louis-Philippe of France, *x*, 41.1
  erects second-class Egyptian obelisk
    in Paris 19
Lucius Verus, Emperor, letters of 46
Lutheranism, Catholic enquirer from 68
Lycia 34

Magdalene College, Cambridge 37
Magna Graeca ware 15
Mahmoud II of Turkey 29
MAI, CARDINAL ANGELO 42-56
  birth at Schilpario in Lombardy 42-3
  attends episcopal seminary at
    Bergamo 43
  studies with Jesuits at Colorno
    in Parma 43
  Professor of *Belles Lettres* at Naples 43
  works at Orvieto and is ordained
    priest 43
  studies classics and Hebrew 43
  Napoleonic law requires him to return
    to Milan in his native Lombardy 43
  Doctor of the Ambrosian library 43
  discovers, collates and
    transcribes palimpsests 44-50, 44.1
  immense discoveries of lost
    classical works 44-50
  selected by Consalvi and Litta
    as Vatican Librarian 46
  collates manuscripts found
    in Ambrosian and Vatican
    libraries 34, 46-47
  discovers Cicero's *De Republica*
    in palimpsests 47
  habitually shows Vatican Library
    treasures to visitors 48
  appointed Secretary of
    Propaganda 48
  appointed Cardinal 48
  re-establishes Vatican Press 48
  has new types cast for
    publishing writings in Latin,
    Greek, Arabic, Syro-Chaldaic,
    Armenian 48
  transcribes the *Codex Vaticanus* 48
  <u>Publications</u> 49-50
    Scriptorum veterum nova collectio
    Classici scriptores ex codicibus
     Vaticanus editi
    Spicilegium Romanum
    Nova Patrum Bibliotheca
    Edition of the entire Greek Scripture
    (published posthumously
     after being edited by team
     of scholars)
  British Royal Society of Literature
    awards him its Gold Medal 49
  foresees death 51-2
  final illness and death 49
  provisions of will 51
    personal manuscripts left to
     Vatican Library 51
    Library sold at half its value
     to Vatican Library 51
    enriches poor of his native village
     with an endowment 51
    ecclesiastical plate and furniture
     given to his native village
     church 51
    monument erected in titular church
     of St Anastasia with inscription
     from own draft 52-3
    books kept together in
     Vatican Library 51
  <u>Physical characteristics</u>
    dignified intellectual features 54
    noble forehead 54
    deep burrowing eyes 54
    knitted brows arising from
     short-sightedness 54
  <u>Personal characteristics</u>
    modesty and humility 53
    simplicity of life 53
    affable and kind 54-5
    diligence and persistence in
     scholarship 53
    scrupulous in religious
     observance 53
    availability 48
    lack of superciliousness 54

INDEX

learning and genius always
  discernible 55
transcribes all work in
  own hand 50
fine and noble prose style 55
Wiseman rejects claim that
  he was restrictive in granting
  scholars access to Vatican
  manuscipts 55
Vatican Library crowded with
  scholars during his tenure 55
valued hard work in subordinates
  and others 56
Manchester 30
Marco, Cardinal 2
Marco Polo 6
Marcus Aurelius, Emperor
  letters of 46
Massimo Villa in Lateran Palace 33
Matranga, Abbate, assistant
  to Cardinal Mai 50
Matthew, Antony xii
Maxentius, Roman Emperor 23
Maynooth, St Patrick's College at 37
Menotti, Ciro 8
Metternich, Prince Clement de 11.2
Mezzofanti, Cardinal Giuseppe 37-9
Michaelangelo Buonarroti 21
Milan 43, 46-7
Mirari Nos, which condemns aspects
  of de Lamennais' writings
Modena, Grand Duke of 8
Modernism xvi, 65
Monchaca SJ, Fr 43
Monte Porzio 27, 27.1
Moore, Thomas, Irish poet, 35, 35.1
Morocco, Emperor of 72
Moroni Signor 4.1
Moses 19
Mozzi, Fr Luigi 43
Münich 33
Murano 4
Museo di Roma xi
"My Saviour's Tomb", poem
  by Père Geramb 36

Naples, Acton famiy at 39
Naples, king of (see Ferdinand II)
Naples, Museum of 15
Napoleon I of France v-vi, xiii.1, 43
Napoleon, Prince Lucien 16
Napoleonic "reforms" in Rome xiii
Napoleonic Law 43
Nero, Roman Emperor 23
Neville, Dr, of Magdalene College
  Cambridge 39
Newburgh peerage in Scotland 3
Newcastle 30
Nicassio, Susan Vandiver xiii
Nicholas I, Emperor of Russia
  presents to Pope quantity of
    malachite for rebuilding
    San Paulo fuori le Mura,
    and vase made of this 61
  allows persecution of
    Catholic subjects,
    especially Poles 61-2
  concerned about personal
    security on visit to Rome 62
  conference with Gregory XVI
    62-5
  ameliorates treatment
    of Catholic subjects 65
Nicols, Aidan, OP xvii.1
Niebuhr, Berthold Georg 56
Nielsen, Frederick
  Danish historian vii.1, xii, xviii
Nietzche, Frederick xix
Nile River 19
Nova Patrum Bibliotecha of Mai 49

Odescalchi, Cardinal Carlo 2
O'Gorman, Edward viii.1
Orvieto 43
Oscott College *front.*
Ottoman ambassadors to
  London and Paris 29
Overbeck, Johann Friedrich
  33-4, 67.1
Ovid, Publius Ovidius Naso
  31, 31.1
Oxford Dictionary of Popes vi

Pacca, Cardinal Bartolomeo
  Dean of the Sacred College 2
pagan burial customs 17-18

palaestra, mosaic in Lateran
Palace of 23
Palermo 41
palimpsests 44-50, 44.1
Papacy, alternation of seculars
and regulars for 4
Papal encyclicals xi-xii
Papal infallibility vii
Papal recognition of de facto
governments 13
Papal States,
revolution of 1831 in
Papi in posi, catalogue of photographic
exhibition of popes xi.2
Paradiso of Dante 33
Paris 20
Parma, Duchy of 43
Paroles d'un Croyant xix, 65
Pauline chapel in Vatican 28
Perugia 67
Perugino, Pietro 67.1
Pergamum 23
Peters, Herman animal painter 21
Petrarca, Francesco 47
Philo Judaeus, fragments of 46
Piedmontese occupation
of Rome in 1870 xiv
pifferari, Abruzzian
bag-pipes xv.2
Pincio
adorned with Egyptian obelisks
by successors of Pius VI 18
Pittsburg, bishop of 62
PIUS VI ix, 43
erects Egyptian obelisk
in the Quirinal palazzo 18
permits Society of Jesus to be
re-established in Naples 43
PIUS VII front., ix, 4, 5.1, 6, 20, 57, 63
Wiseman's veneration for 75
PIUS VIII
respect of Wiseman for 75
PIUS IX
appoints Wiseman to restore
English hierarchy front.
Pliny, Gaius Plinius Secundus 23
"Plura inter collegia" whereby Leo XII
granted Umbrian College buildings to
Irish College 69
Poggio Bracciolini, Giovanni
Francesco 47
Polynesia ix
Ponte d' Asso 16
Pontemolle 58
Porta Maggiore
ancient tomb discovered within
28-9
Porziuncola 67
Post Office in Rome 9
Portrait of Gregory XVI acquired
by Emperor Alexander II when
Czarovitch 61
Propaganda Fide ix-x, 60, 73
Prussian court's patronage of
science in Rome 34
Purgatorio of Dante 33

Quirinal Hill 18
Umbrian College on 69
Quirinal Palace, viii, 5

Railways in the Papal States vii, 31
Raphael 21-2
Rationalists xvii
*Recollections of the Last Four Popes
and of Rome in their Times* front
Redschid Pasha, Ottoman
ambassador in London 29
Republics of South America x
Restoration of the English
hierarchy front., 69
Reumont, Dr 58
Richmond, Surrey 39
Riddell, Bishop 2
rite of papal consecration 7-8
Roman costumes xv.2
Roman forum, restoration of 26
Roman streets, seen by Romans
as part of houses on which
they stand xiv
romanticism xvii
Rome, character of people of xiii
lament for Old xiv-xv
Russell, Very Rev Dr 27
Russia, Catholics of 61-5

INDEX

Sacred College of Cardinals 40
St Agatha in Suburra, church of 70
St Angelo, fort of 8
St Alphonsus Liguori
 canonised by Gregory XVI
  in 1839 30
 nephew carries his banner at
  canonisation of 30
St Anastasia, church of 52
St Andrew, chapel of
St Augustine of Canterbury 5
St Augustine of Hippo,
 manuscript of *Commentary
 on the Psalms* of 47
St Charles Borromeo 44
St Columbanus 44
St Ephrem, edition of 48
St Gregory the Great,
 monastery of 5
St John-the-Beheaded,
 confraternity of *xiv*
St Lawrence, basilica of
 cemetery completed, and
  public burying there made
  mandatory 26
St Paul, Gothic version of
 letters of 46
St Paul-without-the-Walls, basilica of
 (see San Paulo fuori le Mura)
St Peter Damian *v*.1
St Peter, first epistle of *xi*
St Peter's Basilica 7
 decorated and illuminated
  for a canonisation 30
 altar of Blessed Sacrament of *xx*
St Peter Orseolo *v*.1
St Romualdo, founder of the
 Camaldolese Order 5
St Thomas Aquinas *v*
St Wolstan 29.1
Salop 41
San Marco, Venice,
 library of 6
San Michele a Ripa 66
San Michele di Murano
 Camaldolese monastery of *v*
San Paulo fuori le Mura *xi*.1
 Emperor Nicholas I's gift
  of malachite for 61
 consecration of *xi*, 61
Santa Maria degli Angeli 67-8
Santa Maria Maggiore 28
Scarabæi 20
Schadow, Baron von 34
Schadow, sculptor brother
 of above 34
*Scriptorum veterum nova
 collectio* of Mai 49
Scruton, Roger *xix*
secret societies in
 Papal States *xix-xx*
Severoli, Cardinal Antonio 2
Seville Cathedral *front*
Shrewsbury, Earl of 28
Silesia 34
Singulari nos, encyclical
 which *inter alia* condemns
  Paroles d'un croyant
  by Lamennais *xi*
Sixtine Chapel 21
slave trade and slavery
 condemned by Gregory XVI
  in encyclical of 1839 29
Society of Jesus *xi*, *xviii*, 29
Solicitudo Ecclesiarum *x*, 12
Sophocles, statue of 22
South America, Spanish rule
 in 2
Spain, King of (see Ferdinand VII)
Spicilegium Romanum
 of Mai 49
Statius, Publius Papinius 76
steamboats on Tiber 31
Sybilline books, text of
 6th & 14th of 46
Syriac, Old (Syro-Chaldaic) 48, 52

Talbot, Lady Gwendolen (see
 Princess Borghese)
Tarpeian Rock, German
 scientific association on 34
Tarquinii 16
Taquisara, novel
 by F. Marion Crawford *xv*.3
Termini orphanage
 (at *Thermae* of Dioceletian) 66

Testaments, New, manuscripts
of 44
*The Commonplace Book of
Monsignor A.N. Gilbey* xviii.1
"The Dunce of the College" 69-70
Theiner, Fr Augustin 34
Throckmorton, Elizabeth (see Acton)
Throckmorton, Sir Robert 40
Tiber, capital works carried out
at mouth of 26
Tivoli xi, 12, 19.4
Todleben, Eduard Ivanovich 9
Torre di Qunta 58
Tosti, Cardinal Angelo
Gregory XVI's Treasurer 23, 66
*Transactions of
Academia of Cortona* 15
*Trionfo dello Santo Sede e della Chiesa
contro gli assalti dei novatori
combattuti e respinti colle
stese loro armi* xvi-xvii
Tristia of Ovid 31, 31.1
*Triumph of the Holy See and of the
Church against the Assaults of the
Innovators* xvi-xvii
Turkish ambassadors 29
Turks 29
Tusculum 5

Ulphilas, Gothic version of
scripture by 46
Ultramontane movement xi
Umbria, earthquakes in 66
uncial letters 45
United Italy with Rome as its capital,
declaration of xiv
Ushaw College *front.*

Valence, where Pius VI
died in exile v
Vatican Palace
restoration of Pauline chapel in 28
Library of 44, 46, 48, 52
Museum of 19
inauguration of Etruscan &
Egyptian collections in 18
Egyptian obelisk before 18
gallery of paintings in 20-1

Veith(Veit) Philip 33
Venerable English College
surrendered as supernumerary
hospital during cholera
outbreak in Rome 27
creates Committeee of Health at
Monte Porzio country retreat 27-8
receipt of collection of maps
hung on rollers 71
receipt of giant medicine chest
from London pharmacy 72
visit of Gregory XVI 71-3
inscription commemorating
Pope's visit to 72-3
patrons & protectors of 6, 73
Venice i
Vincennes 37
Virgil, Publius Vergilius Maro
ancient commentaries on
works of 46
Visitors to Rome xii, xiv-xv
Volterra 15
Vulci 16

*Walks in Rome and Days
near Rome*, travel guide
by Augustus Hare xv.2
Walsh, Bishop 31
Ward, Mrs Humphrey xv
Waterloo, battle of 35
WELD, CARDINAL THOMAS,
at conclave of 1831 2
appoints Bishop Riddell as
Secretary at conclave 2
patron of Venerable
English College 73
provides Rome apartment
for Wiseman's lectures
in 1835 74
death 3
Westminster School 39
Whinder, Rev Richard
acknowledgments
Introduction by i-xx
"Whiskers of Géramb" 35
WISEMAN, CARDINAL NICHOLAS
birth in Seville *front.*
parents *front.*

INDEX

pupil at Ushaw College *front.*
doctorate in theology *front*
Professor of Oriental Languages *front.*
recalls fear of Roman insurrection
  in 1831 8-10
involved in organising Committee
  of Health during plague 27
shows parties around the
  Vatican Libary 48
frequent contact with
  Cardinal Capellari as Prefect
  of Propaganda 73
visits earthquake zone
  in Umbria 66-7
made papal chamberlain 71
organises Gregory XVI's visit to
  Venerable English College 70-1
gives lectures in Cardinal
  Weld's Roman apartment 74
appointed by Gregory XVI
  as co-adjutor to Bishop Walsh
  in 1840 with residence
  at Wolverhampton 30-1
lectures on Catholic Faith
  in London *front*
appointed by Pius IX as first
  Archbishop of Westminster *front.*
granted Cardinal's hat *front.*
views and publications
  believes outsiders too presumptious in
  having views on how Pope should
  govern temporal realm 20
  believes no monarch more
  conscientious than Gregory XVI 26
  explains difficulties in knowing
  the inner life of individuals 24
  claims general public has lack of
  interest in internal affairs
  of foreign states 24-5
  compares England and Papal states
  in respect of material and
  artistic achievments 31-2
  notes ability of Rome to
  nurture men of genius 32
  believes that art in Rome
  clings unreasonably to
  classical style 33
  instances Gregory XVI's

  personal encouragement for
  his literary and ecclesiastical
  endeavours 1, 75
  personal affection for
  Gregory XVI *xx*, 75-6
  literary publications, *front*
  prayer for conversion of
  England Annex B
Wolverhampton 24

ZURLA, CARDINAL PLACIDO
  Camaldolese monk 6
  publishes book on Marco Polo
    and early Venetian travellers 6
  intimate friend of Dom Mauro
    Cappelari (later Gregory XVI) 6
  named Cardinal in 1823 6
  Vicar of Rome 6
  Protector of the Venerable
    English College 6
  dies in Sicily in 1834 6

First volume of
Wiseman's Recollections of the Last Four Popes and of Rome in their Times
PIUS THE SEVENTH
with an Introduction by Antony Matthew and a full index

"There is nothing too good for us to give the English Catholics," said Pius VII. A massive gold chalice, set with emeralds, diamonds and pearls, and cruets, bell and paten, all of the finest gold, were his gift for the Pro-Cathedral of St Mary Moorfields which in 1820 had recently been completed for the Catholics of London. His advisers protested that they were his most valuable items of church plate. But he insisted on their being sent.

From the age of sixteen, Cardinal Wiseman knew Pius VII. He was received by him as one of a tiny band of English students who arrived in Rome in 1818 to reopen the Venerable English College. This had been forcibly closed and sacked by the occupying French army twenty years before. Why Pius VII had such a high opinion of English Catholics, and even of the Prince Regent and other Englishmen, is a fascinating aspect of Wiseman's story, and explains why the Royal Collection acquired its fine portrait of Pius VII by Sir Thomas Lawrence.

Pius experienced wild changes of fortune during his long reign. Called to be Sovereign Pontiff from the retired life of a Benedictine monk, he was brutally expelled from Rome in 1809, and imprisoned on the orders of Napoleon. How he eventually overcame Napoleon, and how his Secretary of State, Cardinal Consalvi, used diplomatic skills in London and at the Congress of Vienna to effect a triumphant and popular restoration of his rule in the Papal States, is a tale worthy of Wiseman's skill as a novelist. The early years of his reign before his imprisonment, and the eight years after his restoration, were among the most fruitful periods in the history of the Papal States.

In his account Wiseman gives us his own views on the Church and the world soon after he was entrusted with restoring the English hierarchy. But he also reveals how this gentle but resilient Pope, with his ability to attract the love of devoted advisers, and his trust in Divine Providence, could combine benevolent and effective temporal rule with deep personal piety and holiness.

146 pages £8.99

ISBN 1874037 17 5

Second volume of
Wiseman's Recollections of the last Four Popes and of Rome in their Times
LEO XII AND PIUS VIII
with an Introduction by Antony Matthew and a full index

Cardinal Wiseman published his recollections of Leo XII and his successor Pius VIII in 1858. It was eight years since he had been the papal choice to restore the English hierarchy. The two popes had reigned for little more than seven years in the eighteen twenties. Their policies were frequently misunderstood, and their true worth and significance were usually only fully understood much later.

Leo XII succeeded Pius VII. This popular and virtuous pope, by the time of his restoration as ruler of the Papal States, was admired throughout Europe for his courageous stand against Napoleon which had cost him five years as the Emperor's prisoner. Leo had other priorities than those of papal temporal rule. He was concerned about the decline in moral standards and religious observance which accompanied the intellectual and political changes resulting from "enlightenment thinking," the French revolution and the Napoleonic wars. Wisemen shows how Leo was ready to risk unpopularity to reestablish the See of Peter's spiritual and moral leadership of Christendom. Leo XII has been simplistically attacked as a reactionary. That is why Wiseman's account of his short reign is so important. He actually knew Leo, and owed much of his future advancement to his personal encouragement. A careful study of Leo's pontificate shows how the seeds of the great nineteenth century revival of Catholicism owe much to his courageous and self effacing foresight.

The accounts of the two reigns cover two papal conclaves, the highly successful Jubilee of 1825, the first for fifty years—convoked against the advice of the Papal advisers and many of the crowned heads of Europe, and Catholic Emancipation in Britain which was finally achieved under Pius VIII. This was the background to the appointment of the first English cardinal since the reformation.

The work is suffused with Wiseman's love of the Eternal City, the great ceremonies of the church, and the world of high intellectual scholarship in ecclesiastical, classical, linguistic, biblical and archaeological learning, in which the future cardinal was able to make his personal mark.

162 pages   £9.99
ISBN 1 874037 18 3

Recent books

THE CARDINAL'S SNUFF-BOX

A villa in the Italian lake district, in a summer of the late 1890s; a castle in a garden, a lake, and snow-capped mountains in the distance; a beautiful woman glimpsed a few times in the past; a young aspiring novelist.

In this elegant novel Henry Harland has combined an amusing and observant narrative with an exploration of opposing religious and philosophical views of life, which are ultimately reconciled by a pig, a storm, and a cardinal with the help of his snuff-box.

170 pages £8.99

SET THE ECHOES FLYING
AN ANTHOLOGY OF POEMS, SONGS AND HYMNS

This includes most of the favourites of England, Ireland, Scotland, and Wales. Five hundred years of pieces to inspire, amuse and comfort. A bedside book for all ages, and acknowledged the best of its kind since General Wavell's *Other Men's Flowers* published in the 1940s.

272 pages   *with illustrations by Mary Tyler*   £10.99

Other titles

Pilgrims to Jerusalem: accounts of visits to the Holy Land	£12.99
Robert Hugh Benson: Confessions of a Convert	£5.99
Elizabeth Butler—Battle Painter: Autobiography	£7.99
G K Chesterton: Autobiography (2nd edition)	£11.99
G.K. Chesterton: A Short History of England	£9.99
William Cobbett: A History of the Protestant Reformation	£9.99
F Marion Crawford: The Heart of Rome (novel)	£7.99
Hugh Dormer DSO : War Diary	£7.99
Bernard Holland: Memoir of Kenelm Digby	£6.99
Helen Jackson: Ramona (novel)	£8.99
Antony Matthew: Pearl of Great Price	£5.95
John Henry Newman: Collected Poems & Dream of Gerontius	£8.99
Coventry Patmore: The Bow set in the Cloud (his best critical writings)	£8.99
Francis Thompson: Collected Poems	£9.99

If you have difficulty in purchasing Fisher Press titles from bookshops you may acquire them direct from Fisher Press, Post Office Box 42, Sevenoaks, Kent, TN15 6YN. Telephone/Fax 01732 761830.